BEYOND
THE CRITTERS

Considerations for Managing and Leading State Fish and Wildlife Agencies

Dwight Guynn, PhD

I would like to thank the staff of the
Association of Fish and Wildlife Agencies'
Management Assistance Team
for their assistance throughout
the development of this book, and for
their financial support of its publication.

ISBN: 978-1-59152-194-5

Published by AFWA's Management Assistance Team

For more information, contact AFWA's Management Assistance Team,
698 Conservation Way, Shepherdstown, WV 25443

You may order extra copies of this book by contacting AFWA's Management
Assistance Team, 698 Conservation Way, Shepherdstown, WV 25443

sweetgrassbooks
an imprint of Farcountry Press
Produced by Sweetgrass Books
PO Box 5630, Helena, MT 59604

 Produced and printed in the United States of America.

20   19   18   17   1   2   3   4

Table of Contents

Preface

This book has been thirty years in the making. It is my attempt to capture the salient points of what I learned over my career working with state fish and wildlife agencies. I wrote this book at the urging of many so that the next generation of fish and wildlife professionals could avoid the accumulation of "scar tissue" while learning what it took me so many years to amass. I enjoyed ten years with the Montana Department of Fish, Wildlife & Parks, then spent the last fifteen years of my career working with the Management Assistance Team (MAT). MAT is a small group that's essentially an in-house consultancy and training arm of the Association of Fish & Wildlife Agencies, serving all fifty state fish and wildlife agencies. My experiences working with MAT and all the state fish and wildlife agencies have been the highpoint of my career and given me a perspective without which I could not have written this book.

The idea for this book came about during my last few years before retirement as I reflected upon what I wish I had known early on in my career. I hope these insights help others in state fish and wildlife agencies as they continue their conservation work. Also, I believe that anyone contemplating a career in wildlife management will benefit from this glimpse into the real world of life in a state wildlife agency and what it takes to be successful.

In addition, many interested citizens care deeply about what their state fish and wildlife agency does and how it functions. This book can provide them with a deeper understanding of how these agencies best function. I decided to write this book because there is nothing like it in the literature today. What I have put in these pages is unavailable in any single publication.

This book is divided into seven chapters. The chapters are arranged like a funnel, starting with the narrowly detailed specifics of managing a state fish and wildlife agency, then expanding to the broader subjects of changing the organization, leadership, and a look at the future of fish and wildlife management. Chapter One, "Work Plans–A Multifaceted Tool You Can't Do Without," deals with the day-to-day tools of how to (1) manage for accountability, (2) build a defensible budget, (3) implement a budget cutting process when needed, and how to effectively provide direction for a large agency using this tool.

Chapter Two explores the interdependencies within a state fish and wildlife agency and how making one-dimensional decisions about only a part of the agency without considering the interactions with other parts of the agency can lead to unintended consequences. Each successive chapter gradually progresses to the broader perspectives of effective leadership, ending with Chapter Seven, "A Look Ahead," where I share my thoughts on factors affecting wildlife management today and what they portend for state fish and wildlife agencies.

The journey of writing this book was much longer and harder than I expected. I spent over three years from beginning this project to its final publication. Along the way, many people helped and encouraged me in this effort. I want to thank first my wife, Sally, without whose support and initial editing I would never have seen my way to publication. There have been so many other people's positive influences that I cannot list them all. I will list just a few that have helped the most. Jim Flynn was the first state fish and wildlife agency director for which I had the privilege of working. Other state fish and wildlife agency directors (past and present) who have influenced me greatly are John Cooper, Ken Haddad, Steve Wilson, Glenn Normandeau, John Arway, Dave Chanda, Terry Crawforth, Corky Pugh, and Gary Doxtater. On the national scene, Steve Williams, former Director for Kansas, former Chief of the U.S. Fish and Wildlife Service, and current President of the Wildlife Management Institute, and Max Peterson, Chief emeritus of the U.S. Forest Service, and former executive director of the Association of Fish & Wildlife Agencies, have both been major influences on my career and my perspective. I would be remiss if I did not mention also Marty Linsky and Hugh O'Doherty with Harvard's Kennedy School of Government, both of whom deeply shaped my thoughts on leadership.

I want to thank the members of the Association of Fish & Wildlife Agencies' Management Assistance Team for their support and interest in this book and their support in its publication.

I would also like to thank the reviewers who gave unselfishly of their time and talent to correct my mistakes and oversights. Reviewers include Steve Williams, Dave Chanda, Marty Linsky, Chris Smith, Judy Stokes, Steve Webber, Anita Guynn, Verlyn Ebert, Ken Haddad, Mike Fraidenburg, Max Petersen, Greg Moore, Corky Pugh, John Arway, and Ron Regan. As usual, any lingering missteps are mine alone.

CHAPTER ONE

Work Plans—A Multifaceted Tool You Can't Do Without

The director of one of my favorite fish and wildlife agencies frequently complained that "directing this agency is like herding butterflies!" His observation succinctly voices the difficulty of steering a large government agency on a strategic course. But it's doubly challenging for fish and wildlife directors because their employees are scattered far and wide, often working from remote offices and in field conditions that tend to foster "independent thinking." Also, wildlife agencies operate in a fluid environment—just when you've gotten all the butterflies moving in the same direction, some ecological or socio-political situation arises that requires steering a new course. Over the twenty-five years since I first heard that director's complaint, I have had the opportunity to consult with many state fish and wildlife agencies across the nation. The frustrations that beset that director a quarter century ago still plague many agency directors today.

How *do* you direct an agency of 250 to 1,000 or more employees when they are deployed all over the state, each focused on their individual projects? Obviously, it's not practical to call each employee every Monday morning and tell them what to do. Emails are easily ignored. All too often, the tools simply are not in place to enable the director to effectively guide and manage the agency.

I'm convinced that the most important, over-arching management tool is the annual work plan. A good work plan is versatile, like a Swiss Army knife, with features that will help you bundle tasks into projects, set priorities, make budgeting decisions, and track progress through mid-year variance reports and end-of-year reports. Work plans are so important; they are the sole focus of this first chapter. In the following pages, I explore how to create work plans, how to unlock their useful features, and how to use them to direct your agency or, on a smaller scale, your team with a clear, unified sense of purpose.

The Annual Work Plan

To effectively direct a large group of people such as agency staff, you must: 1) **define** the desired end results, 2) **delegate** the accomplishment of those ends to others, and 3) **track progress** to ensure that the results are achieved. An annual work plan accomplishes all three of these steps. Let's look at each of them a little closer.

Defining End Results—Who is Responsible for What

The upper administration of an agency is responsible for explaining the big picture and setting overall agency direction, and for defining the desired end results. Usually, the desired results are defined with input from the public and the staff since the open and free exchange of thoughts produces the best ideas. Top-level agency managers and their staff then describe the work processes that will be used to achieve the end results. Finally, the managers assign the work to the employees who will produce those desired results.

Delegating Work

The best tool for delegating is a written document for each bundle of work. The bundles of work are often called projects. The document describing a bundle of work is a *work plan*. This document must include several things: 1) the budget and other resources such as personnel required to accomplish the work, 2) the person responsible for the overall work effort, 3) a description of *how* the work will be done, 4) deadlines for accomplishing various parts of the work, and 5) an explanation of how the work relates to the agency's strategic direction, that is, its goals and objectives. (I discuss how to align work processes with an agency's goals and objectives in Chapter Two, in the Work Processes section under the Organization "blade" in the Helicopter Model; see page 42.)

Delegating Work Through Work Plans— The Five Rs

Many of the problems associated with delegation of work relate to wrong assumptions and misunderstandings between the delegator and delagatee about exactly what will be done, when, by whom, within what sideboards, and using what resources. Work plans clarify all of this in writing. Think of the process of delegation as the five Rs:

Results—What end results are to be achieved (What does success look like?)

Resources—Exactly what resources—money, staff time, etc.—will be made available for achievement of the results?

Restrictions—What are the sideboards or restrictions on the means used to accomplish the work? When will it be done? What is not permissible and what authority level is granted?

Review—What will be the review process for assessing the work accomplished and the results achieved? Will the supervisor visit the worksite to view the achievements? Will survey and inventory data be used, etc.?

Rewards—What will be the rewards for the individual(s) responsible for the work? This includes both positive and negative rewards, for example, a certificate of recognition or a day off with pay could be rewards for successful accomplishment of end results. Note that rewards for successful completion of a project should be more than "You *get to keep your job.*" However, if an employee does not complete the work, then sanctions like leave without pay or a letter of reprimand could be used.

The first two Rs incorporated into work plans clearly state work to be done (the *what by when*), *who* is responsible, the *resources available*, and the end result of this work effort. Unfortunately, too often the other three

Rs (Restrictions, Review, and Rewards) are omitted. These need to be spelled out in writing so there is no confusion or later dispute as to what was agreed to during delegation.

An important point for supervisors is that answering the questions posed by the five Rs is a negotiated discussion between the supervisor and the employee(s). It is not a one-sided mandate from the supervisor. The employee negotiates how much they can achieve in what timeframe with what resources, etc. It is a two-way agreement that both the supervisor and employee sign. This agreement is binding on both parties. This type of negotiation using the five Rs prevents any misunderstandings and clarifies the delegation of resources and authority and what restrictions apply. Having such a document prevents most of the problems I have observed with poor delegation practices.

Tracking Progress

Tracking progress becomes much easier once work plans are written. Supervisors can compare work accomplished with the timelines listed in the work plan. If mid-course corrections are needed, they can be made as soon as variations from the planned accomplishments and expenditures in the work plan are noticed. (Using variance reports to track work plan progress is discussed later in this chapter.)

All Agency Work Must Be Included

The most basic building block for aligning budgets and work is an annual work plan *for every funded project* within the agency. Annual work plans must encompass *every funded* project in the agency, including capital improvement projects, which are usually outlined and accounted for in purchasing and contracting documents. These contracting documents can constitute a *work plan* for capital projects. It continues to amaze me that so many state fish and wildlife agencies develop work plans—as required—for all their federally funded projects and contracts for capital projects, but the same agencies fail to use work plans for any other work! When you have work plans only for the federally funded projects and capital projects yet not the other work, then you have half a tool! It's like having the head of an axe without the handle or the handle without the head. You can't reap the many benefits of work plans as a tool for the agency without **all** work being covered by work plans.

Tackling projects without a work plan amounts to throwing money at people and telling them to "go forth and do good things." Managers who don't use work plans typically fall back on two methods to get the work done. First, they give some general direction through position descriptions and verbal communication. Second, they micromanage employee activities and budgets to oversee the work.

Position descriptions do not identify what needs to be done by when. Position descriptions are often out of date and not tied to particular projects. They must not be used as replacements for work plans. Work plans specify **what** will be accomplished and set **deadlines** for their accomplishment throughout the year. Position descriptions focus only on the types of work to be performed. They do not specify how much of each type of work, or more importantly, the results to be achieved.

An example of a good work plan format is shown on the following pages. Fortunately, a work plan need not be long. Two pages should suffice. The information in the work plan is critical. Most of the information is self-explanatory, but two important items bear explaining: *prioritizing work plans and aligning the work plan with the agency's strategic direction*. This information is critical to fully using the tool of work plans in managing an agency.

Work Plan Priorities and Building the Agency Budget

Each work plan should be given a priority in relation to the other work plans for each specific budget. Agency divisions, bureaus, and sections may submit work plans, but some projects reach across such agency boundaries. All facets of the agency should be involved with the director in evaluating and prioritizing these projects that reach across divisions, bureaus or sections.

For example, survey and inventory projects often put wildlife biologists in the lead, but other divisions like law enforcement may also record sightings, conduct counts, and then send the data to the biologists. A project work plan for this type of effort could include law enforcement officers' time and mileage as well as the biologists' time to collate, and evaluate the data and present findings. Another example is the operation and maintenance of wildlife management areas. This might be a primary responsibility of the wildlife division, but if the area includes a lake or stream, then fisheries input would be valuable. And if the area were open to public use, then enforcement and communication personnel would also be involved.

Each division, bureau, or section can submit its work plans in a priority list to the director's office. The work priorities for each division and bureau are the basis for beginning to make budgeting decisions at the overall agency level. The director's office still must make decisions about funding across all units of the agency, and this is when to seek the various managers' input.

After all funding decisions are made, simply adding up the work plans submitted by each division and bureau amounts to the agency's budget! Naturally, the work plans form the basis for discussions between the director's office and division and bureau chiefs about how much is reasonable to request during any particular budget cycle. Budget decisions without work plans usually devolve to struggles of dividing up the financial pie based upon favoritism, who has the strongest support in office politics, who can speak most forcefully, or who can pull in outside influences.

Unfortunately, few agencies derive their budgets through work plans. Instead, they start with a question like, "Given the funding we had last year, what do we want to add in our requests for this year?" Or, "We have to take a budget cut this year, so where do we cut?" This last question is often answered by the seemingly "fair" tactic of cutting every project the same percent. While this may give the appearance of fairness, it avoids facing the real management question: "Which projects are most important?" It also avoids the real problem of answering the question, "Should we cripple a lot of projects or kill a few?" When basing budgets on work plans, these tough management questions are more easily addressed and prioritized work really does drive development of the budget!

Once work plans are written, they **must** be used to build your agency's annual budget request or all the advantages covered in this chapter start to unravel. One agency I worked with spent a year writing excellent work plans all linked to the strategic direction. When it was time to develop the annual agency budget, however, the director called his staff together and launched into the same process the agency had followed for many years—ignoring the work plans. Fortunately, one of the division chiefs realized that unless the budget was built on the work plans, then all the effort of developing work plans would be just another meaningless bureaucratic exercise. When the division chief raised this concern, the director realized he had slipped back into old, familiar ways. He quickly began the new process of working with his division chiefs and using the work plans to develop the budget.

Another advantage to using work plans to drive budgets is that they allow documentation of which projects will be dropped if the budget is cut and what will be added if "extra" funds are available. How so? If you followed the steps outlined above, then you now have a list of all of the agency's work projects in order of their priority. You can also apply this simple concept for earmarked funding by prioritizing all the projects that fall within each earmarked funding source.

Not all agency budgets go before the legislature. In some states, the agency is funded from user fees, with no state general fund appropriation. In other cases, agencies report to a council or commission. A critical point is that the agency director should never take the entire list of 250 to 500 or more work plans, for instance, to the governor's office to incorporate into the governor's budget. Do not present the detailed list of all work plans when testifying on the budget before the state legislature or a commission for budget approval. That is too fine a level of detail for big-picture decision makers. Instead, the director should bundle the work plans into reasonable "chunks" for consideration by the governor's office, commission, and legislature. However, the director now has the details for each chunk ready at hand, prepared to respond to any specific requests for more information.

A common question asked by the governor's office of budget, commissions, and legislatures is *what work will be dropped if the budget is cut by a specified amount*? Instead of fumbling with a general answer and asking for time to come back at a later date with a more specific answer, the director can specify which projects are of lowest priority and, thus, will be cut. This adds greatly to a director's credibility and lets legislators know exactly what "losses" their constituents will suffer if the agency's budget is cut.

Work Plan

1. Project number/Title: _____   2. Fiscal year: _____
3. Brief description of project:

4. Total project costs: $_____ (Include salaries, equipment, supplies, etc.)

          Salaries $_____
       Equipment $_____
          Supplies $_____
             Other $_____

5. FTEs required for completion of this project:
          Position:_____   % of time _____
          Position:_____   % of time _____
          Position:_____   % of time _____
          Position:_____   % of time _____

6. Project Manager:_____

7. Project Priority: _____
    (Note: No two projects can be of the same priority)

8. Describe how this project relates to agency goals and objectives:

9. What are the desired results or outcomes (use measurable outcomes where possible) that will result if this project is completed? What will be the impact if this project is not done?

10. List tasks to be accomplished, including reports, and time frames for completion of each. State as measurable performance standards whenever possible. Also list tasks that cannot be done this year given existing resources.

_____   _____
Project Manager's signature   Supervisor's signature
Date _____   Date _____

Aligning the Work Plan
with the Agency's Strategic Direction

So far, I've discussed work plans as a tool for defining desired results, delegating work, building budgets, and tracking progress (that is, program accountability). There is another critical use for the tool of work plans. It focuses on the question in the work plan, *Describe how this project relates to the agency's goals and objectives*. This question may appear much less important than the budget numbers or work-to-be-done questions. But don't be fooled. Aligning the work plan to the agency's overall goals and objectives is a critical step toward directing the agency in a clear, cohesive direction.

Here's how it works. The agency has developed a strategic direction (often documented in a strategic plan) and ensured that all funded work has a work plan. Each of these work plans must show **how** the work to be done helps move the agency toward its strategic goals and objectives. If a work plan does not relate to the agency's strategic direction, then one of two things is misaligned. Either the strategic plan/direction is incomplete or the work does not support the agency's intended direction and, thus, should not be done.

When the agency director wants to make a change in direction, he or she will likely have to cajole, mandate, or otherwise persuade the staff to make the change. Sometimes a director specifies a particular project be done. Staff members often refer to this as the director's "pet" project(s). When a director unilaterally develops such a project, however, field staff may feel their expertise has been neglected, and they will be less likely to buy in to the work. Setting agency direction is difficult at best and can truly seem like herding butterflies. There is a better way when you have the tools in place through written work plans!

BEGIN WITH "BASE LEVEL" OR "CARRY FORWARD" PROJECTS

A lot of the work done in any agency is repeated each year. For example, law enforcement officers will patrol each year, biologists will conduct surveys and inventory of fish and wildlife populations each year. Therefore, a lot of work plans are "base" or "carry forward" types of projects—work that gets done every year.

IDENTIFY RESOURCES FROM "NON-BASE" PROJECTS OR PROJECTS THAT ARE ENDING

Typically, ten to fifteen percent of the work in any one year is not base or carry forward work. This includes projects that were implemented for a specific length of time, for example a five-year project. If the current year is the fifth year for this project, then it will end at the close of this year. That project's work plan will no longer be viable and the resources committed to that project will be freed up for redirection within the agency. Non-carry forward work also includes any other projects that for various reasons are lower priority; while they may be "nice to do," they are not a necessity. When a project ends or is bumped for higher priority work, the appropriate division/bureau/section chief usually redirects resources as needed. The agency director often has little input and in many cases is unaware of these routine decisions.

Work plans allow opportunities for the director to change this reallocation-decision process and exert influence over the agency's direction. Each year at budget preparation time, the director has the opportunity to direct the agency's future work by using the tool of work plans! The director does this by selecting one or more key issues from the agency's strategic direction to emphasize that year. Then the director sends out a directive that any "new work" proposals for freed up resources must address the chosen strategic direction issues. Employees then use their own initiative and creativity to write the new work proposals for the redirected resources. These new work proposals are prioritized then added to the list of already existing work plans. This total package is used to build the agency budget.

SMALL CHANGES ADD UP

Redirecting ten percent of an agency's efforts in a year may seem inconsequential, but if the same priority is retained in the second and third year, then as much as thirty percent of an agency's efforts can be redirected. This is like turning a supertanker in the ocean. By a matter of degrees, given time and patience, the captain can turn the ship ninety degrees. The same can be said of large government agencies. Using work plans allows the director to steer and affect agency direction while enabling employees to use their own initiative and creativity about how to address specific issues. This approach also avoids the appearance of creating "pet projects." The work plan process also assures program managers that resources will not be taken unexpectedly from their programs to fund pet projects due to whims of the director's office.

This process also ensures that the budget and other needed resources have been outlined for each work plan. When work plans are approved, so is the necessary funding. Thus, when submitting expenditure requests for the work throughout the year, employees are not left guessing whether an individual expenditure will be approved.

BEWARE OF GENERATING A LANDSLIDE OF NEW WORK PROPOSALS

Be careful managing the process for generating new work proposals to allocate redirected funds or as the basis for requesting new funds. It's easy to generate a landslide of "great ideas" and wish lists from employees. Don't fall into the trap experienced by some agencies where the total resources required for the *new work* proposed would consume the agency's entire existing budget! This would leave no resources for the carry forward core work that must be done. Allowing an unlimited number of wish list projects to be submitted each budget year ensures that most will have to be denied. After all, only ten to fifteen percent of the budget will be available for new work.

There are several ways to cap the number of new work proposals submitted. I recommend that each division, bureau, and section receive a limit of some designated percentage of their past year's budget that can be submitted as new work proposals. For example, if a division or bureau's budget the previous year was $10,000,000 and the new work cap was seven percent, then the total for the new work proposals submitted could not exceed $700,000. This process forces each division, bureau, and section to prioritize its wish list for new work and submit only its highest priorities for overall agency consideration.

THE CHALLENGE OF PRIORITIZING WORK PLANS

After your division, bureau, and section chiefs have had their employees prepare work plans for all work, the next step is to prioritize **all** these work plans. The good news is that the critical carry forward and mandatory projects that you know will be funded (such as work mandated by law, basic enforcement, operation of hatcheries, base levels of survey and inventory, etc.) can be set aside from the prioritization process. (If you want to do zero-based budgeting, then these projects can all be included in the prioritization.)

REVIEWING CARRY FORWARD AND NON-CARRY FORWARD PROJECTS
Let's assume that you set aside your carry forward projects and are dealing with work plans that are not required for keeping the agency functioning. Let's say these non-carry forward work plans amount to fifteen percent of the agency's work. Each division, bureau, and section compiles a list of its projects that are not carry forward projects. Both the carry forward and non-carry forward groups of projects are reviewed by the director's office to see if work has been included in carry forward projects that are not really mandatory. Also, I advise that every two to four years the carry forward project lists be reviewed again to determine if they include any work that has become non-carry forward.

PRESENTING NON-CARRY FORWARD PROJECTS
TO THE MANAGEMENT TEAM
Now, you have a list of mandatory or carry forward projects that form your base budget and do not need to be prioritized. Also, you now have a list of non-carry forward projects and new work proposals from all divisions, sections, and bureaus that have been prioritized by the respective division, bureau, or section.

To complete building the budget, the director's office usually holds a meeting of the management team to discuss which of the non-carry forward projects and new work proposals should be included in the final budget request for submission to the governor's office of budget or similar entity. This is best done in a professionally facilitated meeting where cases are made to the management team for project funding and then discussed.

The final part of the meeting is a straw poll of the team members who vote on the non-carry forward projects and new work proposals most in need of funding. An overall priority list is created based on these votes. The director can accept the straw poll results as final on priorities, or use it as information for consideration when making his or her own final decision.

This overall process provides the director an agency budget request consisting of a base amount for mandated and carry forward work and a listing of additional non-critical, existing and new work projects to be done that are prioritized. If the budget is cut, then the director can tell the governor's office of budget, commission, or the legislature what work will be dropped, and conversely, if the budget is increased, what work will be added.

Work Plans as a Tool for Accountability— End-of-Year Reports

In addition to building a budget, work plans provide the tool for individual and agency accountability. To use work plans for accountability, each work plan needs to have an End-of-Year Report. This report is developed at the end of each fiscal year and is the instrument used to account for each work plan's accomplishments and for its financial resources. The End-of-Year Report is a simple accounting that compares three factors: 1) what end results were promised and what was actually produced, 2) what work was supposed to be performed and what work was actually done, and 3) how much of the project's resources (money, full-time equivalent personnel (FTEs), etc.) were used compared to the budget projections. The simple process of using End-of-Year Reports creates the basis for each division, bureau, and section to account for all its work during the previous fiscal year. Summing up these division, bureau, and/or section reports provides the data and basis for the agency's overall annual report.

Many agency annual reports given out to publics, commissions, and legislatures look impressive, with multi-color, slick, printed pages and glossy pictures of fish and wildlife adorning the covers. However, the real accounting for work is often vague and hard to pin down except for a few high-visibility projects. Work plans are a means for **work** or **program** accountability. All state agencies go to great lengths to provide fiscal accountability. These agencies have full-time accountants; they have audits, and a multitude of rules to ensure great **fiscal** accountability. However, there is little **program** accountability in place without the basic building block of annual work plans and End-of Year Reports. **Both** fiscal and **program** accountability are critical to agency effectiveness and accountability.

Work Plans—Checking Mid-Year Progress through Variance Reports

Another important tool based upon work plans is the Mid-Year Variance Report for each work plan. Having at least a mid-year check on progress for all work helps answer questions like: *Is the work being accomplished according to schedule? What is the budget spending record? Is the project underspent or overspent?*

It is much easier to make budget adjustments at the mid-year point than waiting until the end of the year and finding out that there is a major problem. A good example is found in one western wildlife agency with which I have worked over the years. Supervisors request a Mid-Year Variance Report from project managers for each work plan at the middle of the fiscal year. If a project is completely on track, **no report is created** because the supervisor already has the work plan with its projections for expenditures and work accomplishments. When a project is either behind or ahead in work and/or expenditures, then a one-page report is submitted that notes the variances from the original work plan. This is a tool for supervisors to be able to stay on top of project accomplishments and expenditures, allowing them to make mid-year corrections. In this particular agency, some supervisors who had problems with project managers consistently overspending their budgets began requiring quarterly variance reports in order to help their managers do a better job. This worked well. Without work plans for all work to be done in the agency, supervisors are deprived of one of the major tools they can use to better carry out their responsibilities.

Work Plans as the Key to Supervision and Accountability of Personnel

Another facet of annual work plans is their use as an important tool in supervision and personnel accountability. Line managers and supervisors can make great use of such a tool to account for work completion. They check the work plan for what was to be done, by when, and then visit with the employee(s) responsible to check up on progress. It is also important to have a dialogue on whether the expected results/benefits were produced/realized, and whether the work done is effective in providing the desired results. After all, this is the job of supervision and having the tool of a written work plan makes it easier and more structured than checking accountability based upon the whims of each specific manager.

Work Plans as a Tool for Performance Evaluation

Work plans are also a critical tool for assessing personnel performance. If each employee had one work plan, then that alone could serve as the performance evaluation instrument. However, work plans often call for several people working on a project, and employees often have several work plans for which they are wholly or partially responsible. Ideally, when supervisors conduct a performance appraisal, they would have at their fingertips the work plan(s) for which their subordinate is accountable. Essentially, this is the building block for beginning discussions on an individual's performance throughout the year.

The important take-away lesson is to *realize that when you implement work plans, you are changing the way you will build budgets and the way you will prepare annual reports. And you are also providing tools that will change the ways management and supervision are conducted.* Make sure your managers and supervisors understand that they will be expected to change their ways and to actually use these new tools.

Work Plans as a Tool for Controlling the Controlling CFO

Money is power and information is power. When you are the chief fiscal officer (CFO), you have the potential to control both budget expenditures and budget information. This can be a heady experience for the CFO when administrators rely solely on the CFO to tell them what they can buy and how much money they have in each project at any given time. Participating in numerous agency reviews over many years, I have uncovered instances where the CFO actually had de facto control of the agency. In such situations, employees went to the CFO with a "mother may I" approach to their spending and program work. It is a dangerous and seductive habit for both the project managers and the CFO. Sometimes project managers find it easier to let the CFO keep up with the fiscal accounting for each project and the manager just asks the CFO for permission when they need to spend money. The project manager often does not know how much money is left in their project at any point in time. This means the project manager cannot responsibly manage his or her project funds. This responsibility now becomes the purview of the CFO. The problem with this arrangement is that project work decisions involving wildlife work, enforcement work, fisheries work, and so on are now influenced by the CFO who typically has no background or understanding of priorities in these areas of work. While this is certainly not the case in every agency, it is common enough to warrant mention here.

The CFO who has built a power base that depends upon the CFO's superior knowledge and experience using a mysterious "black box" type of state budgeting process and who exercises undue authority in approving requests for spending will most certainly see the implementation of the work plan process as a threat to his or her power. The work plan process opens up the budget building to all in more understandable terms. It also assigns budgets and FTEs to work projects where the project managers know what they have to spend at the beginning of the fiscal year.

It becomes the CFO's responsibility to provide timely accounting of the resources that remain in each project on a regular basis (at least monthly) and in an understandable manner. (This function is often poorly provided by a controlling CFO in order to retain their power over managers). When work plans and timely budget numbers are available in an understandable format, project managers no longer need to go to the CFO and ask, "Can I buy something?"

In reality, the work plan process allows greater accountability for all, and thus, can be reassuring to the CFO. In their defense, CFOs rightly feel responsible for accounting for proper spending of funds. However, where managers have a history of abdicating budget management to the CFO, budget management and accounting will need to be re-emphasized for the managers as part of their responsibilities, and training provided as required.

Work Plan Implementation Challenges

Kotter (1996) lays the groundwork for change initiatives in general, but I will address some specific challenges based upon my experiences with work plan processes.

What Constitutes a Project

Implementing annual work plans in a fish and wildlife agency is a simple concept. But there are some potential pitfalls of which to be aware. For example, once the decision is made for all divisions, bureaus, and sections to prepare work plans for all their projects, the first question typically becomes, "What constitutes a project?" In response, a general guideline might be, "The amount of work for which one person can be held accountable." This does not mean only one person can be working on the project described in the work plan. It means the scope of work and responsibility is such that one person can be accountable for managing however many people are involved in the project. In other words, what is a reasonable span of control?

Work can be divided into projects many ways, and this is best left up to the divisions, bureaus, and sections because, being close to the work, they're in the best position to allocate funding and personnel. That said, do watch out for lumping large amounts of work and money into single work plans as an attempt to have fewer work plans. Why? Because lumping too much together makes the plans so general and diverse that they become much less useful as a budgeting and management tool.

This process should be easiest for your fish and wildlife divisions, bureaus, and sections that are already familiar with preparing project write-ups for federally funded projects. The good news is that your agency work plans should be even simpler than those required by federal mandate.

Work plans for all work makes logical sense. However, I find that it's not as common a practice as one would expect in state agencies. Like most things, just mandating the use of work plans is seldom successful. While the plans can be mandated, the actual **use** of them, along with Mid-Year and End-of-Year Reports, will usually falter without the buy-in of the staff.

Change is Required

Implementation of the work plan process means that staff will need to do things differently than they have in the past. They have spent years learning and using the agency's old ways of doing business and change will not come easily without their buy-in. Work plans will require them to build their budgets, write new work proposals, and account for work in a new and different way. Remember that people support what they help build. Full implementation depends as much on **how** you implement the work plan process as on the actual process details.

In his book, *Leading Change*, John Kotter (1996) suggests an eight-stage process for effecting major change in an organization. Changing the budgeting, supervision, and accountability processes is a classic example of a major organizational change. I highly recommend reading Kotter's book before making efforts to change the process of budgeting and accounting for work. Also, see Chapter Four in this book entitled *Changing the Organization*. Do not overestimate the power of the authority figure to simply force change.

Work Plans for Budget Cuts Decision-Making: Two Conceptual Models

It was 2012. The national economy was a disaster. State and federal agencies were both scrambling to decide how to handle budget cuts. Within the space of a few days, our Management Assistance Team office got calls from two different state fish and wildlife agencies requesting help with establishing a process to make rational budget cuts that were fair and that emphasized keeping the most important work. One agency said that they had made budget cuts several times in recent years and each time a different process was used. They were searching for some consistency and rationale in how this difficult task could best be handled.

Those who have been involved in budget cutting know it's never easy. Processes vary from the *seemingly fair* approach of cutting all programs and projects a set percentage to the practice of arbitrarily selecting candidates for cuts. But across-the-board cuts of a specific percentage amount fails to address the concept that not all projects and programs are of equal importance, while arbitrary cutting is based upon one or a few people's perceptions of the relative importance of the various projects and programs. In addition, employees often interpret even well intended, arbitrary decisions as politically driven or representative of hidden agendas.

For this reason, among many others, many directors and their staff wish to include information from lower level employees in the budget reduction process. The problem is that budget cutting is a very complex process involving a matrix of decisions. Some of the factors to consider include:

- How important is each project compared to others?
- How can each project's importance be fairly ranked against all other projects?
- Is it better to "cripple" a larger number of projects with reductions in resources but retain the projects or to "kill" a fewer number of projects and eliminate them completely?
- What are the consequences of cuts to full-time equivalent positions (FTEs)? For example, is it better to cut an important project that employs only temporary staff and keep a less important project that has permanent FTEs assigned? Most state agencies are very aware that once they cut an FTE, getting it back through the legislative process is difficult at best.
- What are the political ramifications of cutting certain sensitive projects?

The complexity of these decisions makes it difficult to sort through the tangled mass of conflicting factors to reach the best decisions. The desire to gather input from subordinates below the director's office level is confounded by the challenges of trying to develop a process that will prevent turf protecting and get honest input on budget priorities.

As the saying goes, there is more than one way to skin a cat. I won't attempt to illustrate all the possible ways to cut budgets but instead will offer two models for consideration. Model 1 is a very detailed but complicated process that is the most inclusive of lower level staff. Model 2 is one of the simplest. Both of these models use the collective wisdom of division, bureau, and section chiefs and regional manager level staff as well as executive staff. Variations of these processes can be used as needed. These processes are flexible in scale and can be used at an agency-wide level as well as within a specific division, bureau, or section.

The basic component for using each model is a list of work plans for all work listing each project's requested budget resources.

Model 1

Step 1 – List all agency work projects, then remove all carry forward projects from the list

The first step is to list all work projects in one list. Next, identify any projects

Model 1
Decision Process for Budget Cutting

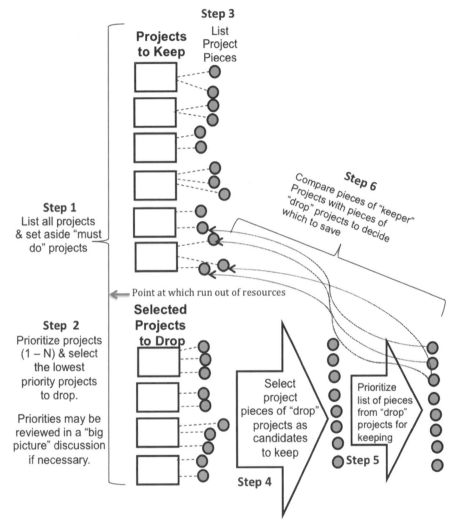

Step 3

Projects to Keep — List Project Pieces

Step 6 — Compare pieces of "keeper" Projects with pieces of "drop" projects to decide which to save

Step 1 — List all projects & set aside "must do" projects

← Point at which run out of resources

Selected Projects to Drop

Step 2 — Prioritize projects (1 – N) & select the lowest priority projects to drop.

Priorities may be reviewed in a "big picture" discussion if necessary.

Step 4 — Select project pieces of "drop" projects as candidates to keep

Step 5 — Prioritize list of pieces from "drop" projects for keeping

Mental Map of the Complex Decision Processes for Deciding Budget Cuts

that are mandatory by law, core to the functioning of the agency, or politically sensitive to the point that dropping them is unacceptable. These are considered 'carry forward' projects and are removed from the list—they will not be considered for cuts. This list of carry forward projects often amounts to up to eighty percent or more of all work projects. A workgroup of division, bureau, and section administrators as well as regional supervisors can help to distinguish the carry forward projects from the other work projects.

The remaining projects that are not carry forward are candidates for being cut. Have a group of staff composed of division, bureau, and section administrators, director's office staff, and possibly regional supervisors prioritize these remaining projects. Before asking the group to prioritize, it is important that everyone has a working understanding of all of the projects on the list.

As an example, some wildlife staff may not fully understand the intricacies of all fisheries projects on the list and vice versa. Also, a specific region's projects may not be fully understood by staff from other regions. Therefore, it may be necessary to verbally summarize the projects to the group. The person in charge of each division's, bureau's, or section's projects can explain each project's costs (including FTEs) and its purpose, and answer any questions from the group. This step works best if you hand out project work plans with dollars and FTE numbers prior to the meeting. The point is that everyone in the room understands the entire list of non-carry forward projects and what they accomplish before beginning the prioritization process.

Respond to questions and requests for clarification as projects are summarized. **Do not** let this *informational* session evolve into a debate of the pros and cons of each project. Remember this part of the meeting is **informational** only.

If public involvement is desired at this step, agencies can use an advisory board or committee that represents their constituencies and ask them to prioritize the non-carry forward projects. This should begin with an information session so that the advisory group can fully understand the projects prior to prioritizing. Also, I recommend that the public involvement group do their prioritization of projects before the agency staff does theirs. This sequence allows agency staff to consider the public input when they do their own prioritization.

Step 2 – Prioritize the non-mandatory projects
To prioritize the non-mandatory projects, the director's office needs to develop criteria to guide the ranking process. This is usually done by the

director and his/her management team. Criteria typically include such things as "bang for the buck," relation to high priorities for the agency, probability of achieving outcomes desired, etc. A few cautions here:

1. Relate project priority to the agency's priorities, which are often stated in a strategic plan or at least in species-specific statewide plans.
2. Don't use more than about half a dozen criteria when prioritizing. People cannot mentally retain more than that number of things at one time when comparing projects.
3. Don't succumb to the temptation of using numbers to weight criteria. I used a matrix numbering system for a couple of years with a state agency and afterward asked them how it was working for them. They confessed that they subjectively knew the relative importance of different projects and so "fudged" the criteria numbers to get them to come out like they wanted. The point is that while math is very precise, the numbers assigned in any weighting process for criteria are still subjective.

DANCE OF THE DOTS

Once criteria are decided upon; gather the project evaluators in a room. This may be a group of stakeholder representatives or it may be a group of decision makers such as director's office staff, regional supervisors or their equivalent, and division, bureau, and section chiefs or their equivalent. Keep the group to no more than about twenty or it will be too cumbersome to manage. Put the list of non-mandatory projects on flip charts on the walls of the meeting room. Total up the number of projects and give each evaluator the number of stick-on dots (such as Avery™ brand) that equals one-third of the number of non-mandatory projects. For example, if there are seventy-five projects on the list, then each person gets twenty-five dots. This is often referred to as an N/3 process.

Why use N/3? It forces evaluators to make choices. If you give evaluators one dot (vote) for each project on the list, then they could put a dot on every project, ranking them all as the same priority. Conversely, if you give each evaluator only one dot, then they don't have enough dots (votes) to indicate their priorities below first place. Experience has shown that the one-third ratio works best (Doyle and Straus 1982).

The more dots a project receives, the higher its priority. Tell the evaluators that they can place their dots on any projects on the list in any order. Also, they can give a project more than one dot (vote). Give the evaluators a few minutes to decide how to "spend their dots" and then let them go to the flip charts to place their dots (usually on the left margin of the flip chart). In this example, an evaluator may put all of his or her dots on one project if that is the only one he or she feels is important. Or they might put one dot on each of twenty-five projects, or any combination in between.

DOT MANIPULATION

Sometimes evaluators try to manipulate the process by waiting until everyone else has placed their dots, then adjusting the priorities by placing lots of dots on one or two borderline projects. To avoid this, adjust the process as follows. Line up all of the evaluators and have them walk by the flip charts placing just ONE of their dots as they walk by. The line then circles back and each person walks by the flip charts again, placing just one dot. This continues until everyone has placed all of his or her dots. When this is complete, the facilitator adds up the dots and scores the projects from one (with the most dots) in importance to last (fewest dots). The results culminate in a prioritized list of projects for possible elimination from the budget using the collective wisdom of the group.

Typically this straw poll is used by the next higher level decision maker(s) (the director's office or a division, bureau, or section chief) to decide budget cuts. Tell evaluators at the outset whether their straw poll will be used as the final decision for cutting projects or as advice to inform the final decision by the agency decision maker(s) such as the director. It's very important that the group know its decision authority level *prior* to engaging in this process.

BIG PICTURE ISSUES

During the final prioritization of projects, it's important to pause and consider potential "Big Picture" issues that may have slipped through the cracks as people ranked individual projects. Examples of these issues include:

- Interrelatedness of projects: project A is dependent on project B, but project B is now slated to be cut while A is going forward.
- Strategic direction: cutting too many projects in one area might affect a unit or program's overall strategy.

It's best if the evaluators discuss such Big Picture issues immediately, with the flip charts of prioritized projects in front of them. Typically, the facilitator asks the group to raise any Big Picture issues and then lists them for the group to address. If the list is long, the group may need to prioritize which issue to discuss first, in case there is not enough meeting time to discuss all of them.

It is not necessary that the group reach consensus on solutions to Big Picture issues, but it is important that they discuss pros and cons of different approaches. The ultimate decision-maker then can use the collective information of the group's discussion as food for thought when making final decisions.

EARMARKED FUNDING

Most state agencies have special funding sources or earmarked funds that legally can be used only for specific purposes. It's not feasible then to list earmarked funded projects in priority order along with other non-earmarked funded projects. The answer to this problem is simple. Just list projects with earmarked funds separately and then categorize them by funding source before prioritizing. For example, in a wildlife division, all bighorn sheep projects funded by specific bighorn sheep designated monies are listed separately. Then that list of sheep projects is prioritized and top sheep projects are funded down the list until the sheep funding is all allocated.

Step 3 – Listing pieces of dropped projects

An added complexity arises in regard to pieces of projects—should we save a piece of a project that is slated to be cut? Sometimes this conundrum is referred to as a "cripple or kill" decision. Do we cripple projects by making cuts to them while keeping some pieces, or do we kill off the whole project?

If you want group input at the project pieces level, then you must split projects slated for being cut into their respective pieces. Then list these pieces as potential candidates for saving.

Step 4 – Selecting "killed" project pieces as candidates for saving
Once you have listed the candidate pieces to save, you may need to set a
limit on how many of them can be carried forward. Such a limit prevents
the group from listing all the pieces as candidates for saving. Next to each
piece, be sure to list its required resources (dollars and FTEs).

At this point there are three options for deciding which pieces to save:

Option 1 - Many agencies leave this up to the final decision maker to
address these issues. In some agencies, division chiefs and program
managers can go to the agency decision maker to plead their case for
saving part of a killed project, and the decision maker then must decide.

Option 2 - Some agencies use a facilitated group discussion among
administrative staff to address this. The final decision maker is present
and listens to the discussion on each project piece. When he or she
has enough information to make a decision on one project piece, then
the group discusses the next project piece, and so on. The group does
not—and probably cannot—reach consensus on each of these decisions. It is the job of the group to discuss the various viewpoints for
the benefit of the decision maker's information.

Option 3 - If the agency decision maker(s) wish further input from staff,
then you move on to Step 5.

Step 5 – Group prioritization of project pieces to be saved
The group can conduct another N/3 exercise with dots to prioritize the list
of project pieces to be saved. This straw poll gives the decision maker(s)
the collective wisdom of the group: their priorities for saving pieces of
"killed" projects.

**Step 6 – Comparing pieces of "keeper" projects with pieces of "killed"
projects to decide which to save**
Bear in mind that to save a piece of a killed project, the needed resources
must come from the list of keeper projects. There are two ways to decide
how to do this:

1. Each project on the lists of keeper and killed projects can be broken
   into separate pieces of work. Since we are now working at a much
   greater level of detail, the process becomes much more burden-

some and time consuming. Also, the more people involved in this process, the greater the difficulty.

2. If practicable, ask the group to suggest pieces of keeper projects that could be cut in order to free up the resources to save some pieces of killed projects.

The pieces being considered for keeping cannot be funded without "stealing" resources from the higher priority keeper projects. Thus the group must review the pieces of keeper projects to see if any of them are less important than the pieces suggested for saving from killed projects. This final comparison is the last step in making budget cut decisions.

Since the process for Step 6 is complicated, it often does not lend itself well to consensus by large groups of people. The best group size for final decisions in this step seems to be no more than two or three people. This does not mean that the budget decisions cannot be transparent and reasons for decisions given to all who are interested. Also, it does not mean that information and suggestions from other individuals cannot be solicited individually before the small group (or agency director) makes final budget decisions.

If an agency wants to have an administrative group of up to twenty or so involved in this decision step, then I recommend that the group discuss each of the pieces to save from killed projects, starting with the highest priority save piece. Don't ask the group to try to reach consensus—its job is to discuss pros and cons of the importance of piece number one to be saved as compared to the resources needed from the lowest priority piece of the keeper projects. The decision maker is present and lets the discussion continue until he or she has enough information to make a decision. The group then moves to the next piece for saving and discusses it in terms of where the resources can be taken from keeper projects.

Some decision makers are reluctant to make budget cuts when they affect people's very livelihood. There is often a naïve desire by the decision maker for a group of staff to reach consensus and, thus, relieve the decision maker from the burden of making those tough decisions. Model 1 allows the decision maker(s) to intelligently use input from staff, but it does not relieve the decision maker(s) from making the final decisions. It is always tough to make cuts in funding, but that is the decision maker's job.

Model 2

Whew! Did Model 1 seem complicated? It is. It illustrates a maximum involvement of stakeholders and employees in budget decisions, an ideal that can provide many benefits. However, I now want to go to the other end of the spectrum and illustrate one of the simplest models I have seen.

I am indebted to Paul Sihler of the Montana Department of Fish, Wildlife and Parks for the following model. It is one of the simplest yet most effective models I have seen in my twenty-five years of working with state fish and wildlife agencies.

Semantics differ between state agencies. The Montana Department of Fish, Wildlife and Parks is divided into divisions. There is a Wildlife Division, Fisheries Division, Enforcement Division, and so on. Other agencies may call these similar parts of their agencies bureaus, sections, or other similar names. Also, Montana has regional supervisors who manage work in separate geographical parts of the state. Other agencies may not have similar positions or may use different names for them. Review the following model with these semantics in mind—substitute names or similar positions from your own agency as appropriate.

The goals of Model 2 are to:
- Reduce the "gaming" that typically happens with budget reduction exercises.
- Provide a process structure that doesn't penalize those who honestly take a hard look at their budgets and propose sensible reductions.
- Appropriately involve division administrators, regional supervisors, and director's office staff in the process.
- Produce programmatic budget reductions that the agency is willing to implement if necessary.

Process Steps

Model 2 unfolds in eleven steps, as follows:
1. Director's Office staff individually draft criteria for evaluating budget cuts and program priorities, then share and discuss; no decision point needed.
2. Director's Office asks division administrators and regional supervi-

sors to provide a list of their suggested criteria for evaluating proposed budget cuts.

3. Director's Office finalizes criteria for prioritizing work projects and programs. Select no more than six or so criteria because that is the maximum a person can keep in mind while reviewing projects.
4. Director's Office asks divisions to apply the final criteria as each develops a list of its non-carry forward projects or programs ranked in priority from highest to lowest. Each division submits a prioritized list of its non-carry forward projects to the Director's Office. Divisions may want to limit what they offer up as non-carry forward and try to protect as many projects and programs from budget cuts as possible. To counter this natural tendency, it may be necessary to assign each division a quota of total dollars for non-carry forward projects and programs that have to be submitted.
5. Director's Office compiles the list of non-carry forward projects and programs and identifies potential cuts to be made.
6. The potential cuts are then reviewed and discussed at a group meeting or videoconference with division administrators and regional supervisors. The purpose of this discussion is to inform the Director's Office of the administrators' and supervisors' thoughts rather than to arrive at a decision point.
7. Director's Office staff meets with each division administrator individually to solicit any last input on proposed budget cuts for each division. (Do this step at whatever management level budgets are allocated within your agency.)
8. Director's Office revises proposed budget cuts for each division based upon input by administrator, independent assessment by Director's Office staff, and consideration of evaluation criteria and program priorities.
9. Director's Office convenes a facilitated group meeting or videoconference with division administrators and regional supervisors to review and explain proposed budget cuts and discuss impacts.
10. Director's Office decides whether to accept any alternatives to proposed budget cuts. This may occur after the facilitated group meeting.
11. Director's Office finalizes budget cuts and reports to all.

Model 2
Decision Process for Budget Cutting

1.   Director's office staff and management team identify potential criteria.

⬇

2. Director's office request divisions and regional supervisors (if appropriate) to review potential criteria and suggest changes.

⬇

3. Director's office staff finalize approximately six criteria and provide to all.

⬇

4. Director requests divisions to use final criteria and each develop a prioritized list of their non-carry forward projects/programs. (it may be necessary to assign each division a quota of total dollars of non-carry forward projects/programs that have to be submitted.)

⬇

5. Director's office staff receives prioritized lists of non-carry forward work projects from each division and identifies potential cuts

⬇

6. Director's office staff review potential cuts at a group meeting or videoconference with division chiefs and regional supervisors. Purpose is to get feedback for the Director's office.

⬇

7. Director's office staff meets with each division chief individually to review and gather any additional input on potential cuts for their division.

⬇

8. Director's office revises proposed budget cuts.

⬇

9. Group meeting of division chiefs and regional supervisors with Director's office staff where Director's office shares proposed budget cuts and rationale. The group reviews proposed cuts and can propose alternative cuts.

⬇

10. Director's office staff decides whether to accept any alternatives.

⬇

11. Budget cuts finalized.

Adapted from Paul Sihler's Model

Note: While this process can rely on videoconferencing in steps 6 and 9, it is my opinion that it is better to hold a face-to-face group meeting with a skilled facilitator. The interaction and group synergy is greater with this type meeting. Also, there is less opportunity for those with negative opinions to complain out of view of the camera. A skilled facilitator can encourage open discussion to resolve dissenting views. This is much more difficult to achieve in a videoconference.

Summary

Work plans are necessary for **defining, delegating,** and **tracking progress** on work—the three most important processes for directing a large group of employees within an agency. While work plans do not have to be complicated—two pages can suffice—they must cover **all** work within the agency.

Work plans provide a means for delegating work. Using the five Rs process when delegating accomplishment of each work plan can enhance the process of delegation. The five Rs compose a negotiated agreement consisting of:

Results (defining what is to be achieved)

Resources (clarifying what resources will be available)

Restrictions (describing the restrictions or sideboards for doing the work)

Review (delineating the review process to evaluate the work)

Rewards (outlining the rewards for doing the work well)

Prioritizing work plans provides a means for building the agency budget based on the work needs for achieving the agency's end results instead of arguing about who gets what piece of the financial pie. In addition, a list of prioritized work plans provides the basis for adjusting work to decreasing or increasing budgets. The process for using work plans in this manner can be complicated or simple depending on the level of input desired by the agency.

All our publics desire accountability in government, and work plans provide a means for accountability to constituents, commissions, legislatures, and governors. This is accomplished with an End-of Year Report for each work plan that can provide accountability for each employee while also cumulatively providing accountability for programs and the agency as a whole.

Work plans provide a means for the agency director to actually direct the agency. This is done by setting priorities for new work proposals each budget cycle. Work plans are truly a multifaceted tool you can't do without.

Work plans are an essential tool for managing an agency however, in addition to having the tools that work plans provide, all the pieces of the agency must function together flawlessly in order to achieve total effectiveness. This requires a broad understanding of all the functioning parts of an agency and how these parts interact. That is the subject of the next chapter.

Literature Cited

Doyle, Michael and David Straus. 1982. How to Make Meetings Work. The Berkley Publishing Group. New York, NY. 298 pp.

Kotter, John. 1996. Leading Change. Harvard Business School Press. Boston, MA. 187 pp.

Osborne, David and Ted Gaebler. 1992. Reinventing Government. Addison-Wesley Publishing Co. Reading, MA. 405 pp.

CHAPTER TWO

A Model of Agency Interdependencies

Most would agree that managing others at work is no easy task. And it's certainly not a big stretch to appreciate the challenge of managing an entire agency of people, or a region, bureau, or division for that matter. Management's job is to make sure that the work get's done. Implied is that the manager also ensures that the work is done effectively.

If you are in a position to influence the effectiveness of your group's work by leveraging factors like creating a new organizational unit (bureau, division, etc.), moving staff among work units, reorganizing, or any other myriad of actions, then you will find this chapter extremely helpful. It's here that I'll introduce you to a management tool that I call the *Helicopter Model*.

Running an agency comes with political as well as practical challenges. Navigating the political morass is beyond the scope of this book. Political challenges are real, however, and cannot be ignored. The problem is that it's easy to get caught up in the mix of political challenges and the more mundane, practical problems associated with the job of managing within a governmental agency. You may find yourself jumping from crisis to crisis putting out brushfires with no overall direction to your actions. The day-to-day routine becomes so chaotic that it engulfs your every moment. You may then mistake the edge of the rut you are in for the horizon. When this happens it's easy to fall back on default management habits and lose focus on the overall picture instead of seeking more effective ways to manage.

While you can never eliminate all the daily crises, rising above day-to-day immediate demands to really direct the agency is critical to doing a good job of agency management. The Helicopter Model is versatile in that it can be applied to a work unit within an agency as well as to the whole agency. Managers at any level will find it useful.

Management procedures in most government agencies have resulted from a conglomeration of historical habits and from arcane budgeting practices rather than from a well-thought-out process. Employees spend years learning to use the current management processes even though these processes may be very flawed. Most of those on the agency's management team—the senior leadership team, executive team, and so on—have learned well how to use the old way of doing things. After all, that's how they rose up the ranks to be on the management team in the first place. Employees naturally assume a comfort level with what they know, and this enhances their propensity to ignore the flaws in the system. "It isn't that they can't see the solution," said renowned English writer Gilbert Chesterton, "It is that they can't see the problem."

A manager may wish to change things in his or her agency to improve work performance on an organizational level. Interestingly, nearly all managers exhibit a reflex reaction to the need for change. It's a compelling enticement to restructure. Moving the boxes on the "wire diagram" of the agency's organization chart gives the appearance of making substantive change, but it often creates unexpected negative results. The assumption is that restructuring will make things better, but the folly of acting on this assumption is that it precludes analysis of the root problem(s) affecting the agency. Taking action without analyzing and understanding the problems is what I call *uninformed tinkering*.

If a manager resists restructuring, then other attempts to improve the agency may take the form of changing strategies and/or adding new programs. But adding a new program, for example, only ignores the web of old processes already in place that still prevent the agency from successful change. While all these administrative efforts at improvement are well intended, they amount to "tinkering" with the current system. They stand a seventy percent chance of failure (Mourier and Smith 2001).

What is needed is a way to rise above all the daily issues and see the whole landscape of the agency. In other words, we need a way to understand the links that connect all the parts of the organizational landscape. It's also important to understand how each part of the organization affects the other parts. Organizations are really like ecosystems—all the parts are connected, and changing one part creates consequences for other parts of the organization. Failure to understand these linkages and interactions leads to making changes that generate unintended consequences while lowering chances for success.

For example, what might be the links and interactions between the agency strategies, the development and empowerment of employees, agency reward systems, and information flow processes? Wouldn't it be awesome if we could rise above the agency and observe all its parts and how they interact? This would be like a wildlife biologist in a helicopter flying above the habitat and surveying herds of big game animals to diagnose the wildlife population status.

Patterns

Ideally, such a high-altitude view of an agency would provide a model or pattern from which to work. For example, try this simple exercise: On the following page, look at the arrangement of numbers and time yourself for one minute to see how many of the numbers you can pick out in numerical order. Record how many numbers you found in the one minute. If you pick out all thirty-six in numerical order, note how much time it required to finish.

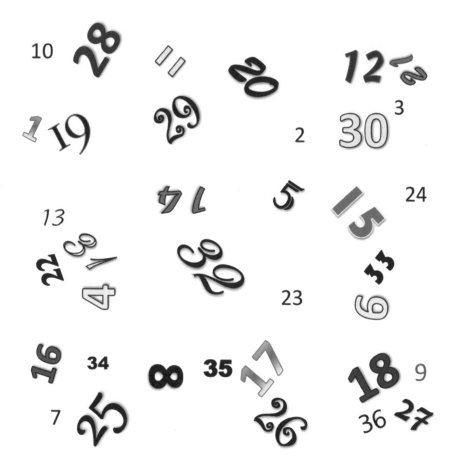

Now look at the same page of numbers, but this time with a tic-tack-toe box overlaying the scramble—the sequence is much easier to see because there's a pattern. The first number is in the upper left box. The next number is in the top center box. The third number is in the upper right box. The fourth number is in the middle left box. This sequence is repeated for all the rows then begins again at the top left box. The sequence runs from left to right and top to bottom.

1	2	3
4	5	6
7	8	9

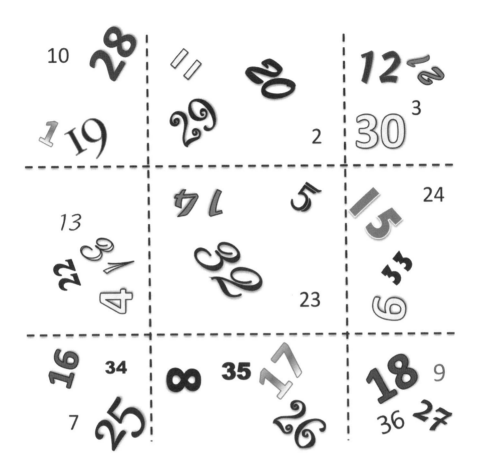

Again, time yourself for one minute and see how many numbers you can find in numerical order.

Were you able to more quickly find the numbers in numerical order once you understood the pattern or model used? This same principle applies in recognizing patterns, models, or connections of the parts of an organization, as I'll explain through what I call the Helicopter Model.

The Helicopter Model

To understand the model better, let's look at each of the six blades of the helicopter in sequence. The blades represent key areas of the agency. Asking sets of probing questions at each blade can help reveal connections and alignments.

1. The Constituents Blade

Always begin by asking questions about the agency's constituents when using this model. It's important to acknowledge that agencies exist for a purpose! That purpose is to serve their constituents. Constituents are people and are subject to change over time. The focus on constituents is defined by asking the questions:

- Who must we serve?
- What are these constituents' needs and expectations of our agency?

This seems simple enough until you look closer. Public agencies tend to say they serve "the public," that is, everyone. But public agencies don't have unlimited resources, so they cannot serve everyone equally. Each agency identifies *whom* (what demographic, recreational base, market niche, etc.) they will serve and *how much* by their allocation of resources

such as staff and dollars. These decisions are made in everyday allocation choices. Earmarked funding, legislative mandates, and some remaining agency freedom drive these choices. The task in this blade of
the Helicopter Model is making these choices explicit as to who will be
served and how much.

A big issue that fish and wildlife agencies have struggled with is the decline in the sales of hunting and fishing licenses. In some state, as little as
three or four percent of the citizens hunt (U.S. Dept. of the Interior, et al.,
2006). Yet these agencies remain dependent on hunting license sales as a
major revenue stream. *Should the agency try to increase its relevancy to the larger
percentage of their citizens or stick with their traditional but declining constituency?*
The strategic decision of whether to try to broaden funding is directly related to the fundamental question of who will be served and how much?

When agencies fail to successfully address the strategic question of
broadening funding sources, it leaves them dependent mostly on traditional hunter- and angler-based dollars. Statutory law has already earmarked
much of this money for such consumptive uses. So the agencies then struggle to sufficiently provide for the expectations of the larger constituency of
non-license buying citizens. Ultimately this is a road to agency irrelevance
as far as those citizens are concerned. The dependence on hunter and angler dollars leads to ignoring, for all practical purposes, the fact that wildlife belongs to **all** citizens—a major underpinning of the North American
Model of Conservation (Geist, V., S.P. Mahoney and J.F. Organ. 2001).

Once the agency's choices are made regarding who is going to receive
services and products, the next step is defining the services and products
that will meet those constituents' needs and expectations. Most agencies
believe that through their daily contact with their constituents, the agency knows the constituents' needs and expectations of the agency. This can
be a dangerous assumption. It's akin to accepting hunters' unscientific
"windshield observations" of deer population numbers as completely accurate information.

Human dimensions and marketing research provide statistically valid
data collection from surveys, focus groups, and other scientific processes. This type of data can be immensely valuable in confirming or reject-
ing assumptions about constituents' needs and expectations. However,
relatively few state fish and wildlife agencies possess the capacity to

gather this type of information or substantially incorporate it into their decision-making. Certainly this is not done on a par with biological and ecological information (Gigliotti, Shroufe and Gurtin, 2009).

2. The Purpose Blade

The second blade of the Helicopter Model is the agency's purpose. The questions posed here include:

- Having determined who the constituents are and identifying their needs and expectations of the agency, what then should be the agency's purpose?
- Is the agency's current purpose sufficient or does it need adjusting? How do you know? If you don't know, why is that?

Since a public agency exists to meet the needs and expectations of its constituents, then the connection between the first two blades (constituents and their needs and agency purpose) is a fundamental one. Based upon refinements in determining constituent needs and expectations, the agency's purpose is also determined or refined. Traditionally, an agency's purpose is expressed as a mission statement. Often it can be found in enabling legislation. If so, is it sufficiently specific for your agency or just a broad general statement?

In the fish and wildlife profession, agency employees sometimes believe they work for the wildlife and that the agency's constituents are really pretty much a nuisance to be suffered. It may be a naïve view, but it's not hard to understand its genesis. Employees holding these views confuse their personal commitments of working to benefit wildlife with the reality of a public agency that citizens support because those publics have expectations and needs they believe the agency will meet.

No trout, bear, deer, turkey, songbird, or other form of wildlife has ever written a paycheck to a fish and wildlife agency employee. By accepting a paycheck, employees are recognizing, de facto, that there are constituents who financially support the agency and the agency employees whose work serves them. The employees' personal commitment to benefiting wildlife coincides with many of the public's desires and expectations of the agency, but that does not mean that the employees work for the wildlife instead of the public.

3. The Methods Blade

The third blade in the Helicopter Model represents methods or strategies selected by the agency to serve its constituents. The central question for this blade is:

- What are the best methods or strategies the agency can employ to meet constituent needs?

If a public agency is clear about the constituency it serves, those constituent's needs and expectations, and clear about the agency's purpose/mission, then it must also design the right methods to carry out the mission. These methods are often called *strategies* for getting the mission accomplished. When implemented, they take the form of major program areas.

The methods follow from the mission, which follows from the constituents' needs and expectations. All three blades (constituent needs, agency purpose, and methods) are connected in this manner. Problems arise whenever a linkage breaks down between these three blades. Broken linkages may take such forms as:

- Constituent values have changed from when the agency was established, but the agency has not changed with its constituents. Example: The majority of a state's population no longer hunts and is focused on other uses of wildlife and conservation in general, but the agency remains focused on hunting and angling as its major products.
- Constituent needs have changed but the agency has not changed to meet them. For example: The spread of chronic wasting disease due to illegal practices on game farms threatens ungulate populations. However, the agency's enforcement efforts still concentrate on catching poachers instead of ensuring game farm compliance with regulations.
- The agency may be clinging to old methods and strategies that no longer serve its constituents as well as they once did. Example: funding strategies for the agency are still focused on hunter and angler license fees and not on funding sources that provide for meeting broader needs. (Note: Just because implementing a new strategy is difficult is no reason not to pursue it.)

4. The Organization Blade

This fourth blade of the model represents how the agency is organized. Organization in this context includes not only the agency's structure but also how the agency's systems and processes are organized. Aligning all of these features is a crucial part of agency effectiveness. Ideally, for maximum effectiveness, each and every part of the organization needs to be **perfectly aligned** to carry out the agency's strategies and fulfill the agency's purpose. This is especially relevant for achieving desired results over the long term.

I've already warned about overreliance on restructuring as the answer to whatever problems exist. Managers are susceptible to restructuring because it is the most obvious change to make, it can be done relatively quickly, and upper level management can mandate it. All are appealing factors, especially when commissions and governors are demanding change.

However, structure is only **part** of the organizing process. There is much more. In fact, there are six key components of any organization that must be aligned in order to achieve optimal effectiveness. The Big Six (FranklinCovey Co., 1995) organizational components for alignment are:

1. The right **decision processes,**
2. The right **structure,**
3. The right **people and training,**
4. The right **rewards system,**
5. The right **information processes,**
6. The right **work processes.**

Alignment of these Big Six organizational components results in each individual component supporting, not impeding, the work and function of all the other components. Think of the correct alignment of an agency as dependent upon fitting together these six organizational components. Let's now look at each of these Big Six organizational pieces individually.

DECISION PROCESSES

Decision processes must align with the other five organizational pieces. The most common problem I find in this area is that budget allocation decisions do not align with priorities as defined in the agency direction

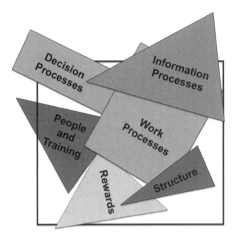

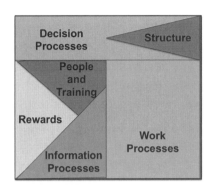

Puzzle of the "Big Six" Organizational Pieces
OUT OF ALIGNMENT

Puzzle of the "Big Six" Organizational Pieces
PERFECTLY ALIGNED

or strategic plan. For example, the budget allocation process in state fish and wildlife agencies often results in accountants having to make de facto management decisions (see Chapter One). When budgeting for a new fiscal year, the process is often based upon how much money and personnel the agency had last fiscal year, then submitting justifications for adding any new requests. Or, in a declining economy, submitting decisions of how much will be cut in order to meet some mandated target for overall budget reduction. The problem is that this approach amounts to the dollars driving the work instead of vice versa! Clearly, when this is the case, the decision processes are not aligned for the agency to be effective.

Strategic direction is set in impressive strategic plan documents. Unfortunately, the plans often are then put away and nothing much different happens in the agency in spite of great expectations and promises made. *Why doesn't the agency implement the changes required to produce the results stated in its strategic plan*? Much of the answer is that the **decision processes** for developing the budget are not aligned with the decision processes for developing the strategic direction of the agency. In other words, write a strategic plan but continue budget decisions the same old way.

There are many ways misaligned decision processes can prevent the implementation of well-thought-out methods and strategies that were developed with public input. Decision processes for purchase of equipment, allocation of time, and many other decisions must be aligned to produce seamless results. How do your agency's decision processes align with desired results?

Marcia W. Blenko and her co-authors (Blenko et. al. 2010) point out the importance of decision processes by arguing that ultimately the value of any organization is no more or less than the sum of the decisions it makes. They recommend six steps to any reorganization that uses decision processes as a major factor for alignment:

1. Identify your organization's key decisions.
2. Determine where in the organization those decisions should happen.
3. Organize the macrostructure around sources of value to clients.
4. Figure out what level of authority decision-makers need (and give it to them.)
5. Align other elements of the organizational system, such as rewards, information flow, and work processes, with those related to decision-making.
6. Help managers develop the skills and behaviors necessary to make and execute decisions quickly and well.

THE KFC EXAMPLE

A corporate example illustrating decision process misalignment occurred a number of years ago with the fast-food chain Kentucky Fried Chicken (KFC). Upper level management had a common goal of providing its customers with quality fried chicken and quick service. However, there was a secondary goal to reduce costs when possible. The decision was made to rate employees' performance at each restaurant based on the amount of fried chicken that was left over at the end of the day, which represented wasted costs.

Of course, employees responded to this decision in predictable fashion. They cooked up chicken only after an order was placed. Every time a customer placed an order, they were told, "It will be about twenty minutes while we cook the chicken for your order." The result was dissatisfied customers because they had to wait so long to receive their order. I remember this debacle from the times I visited my local KFC and repeatedly had to wait for chicken to be cooked. The decision process was a misalignment for KFC. It resulted in great customer dissatisfaction and lost business. It took about a year, but fortunately upper level management finally got the problem corrected by allowing each restaurant manager to decide how much chicken to cook based on each managers' personal experience with demand fluctuations and time of day.

THE NUISANCE WILDLIFE EXAMPLE

An example of decision misalignment for a fish and wildlife agency is what can occur when the agency wants expedient responses to public calls for wildlife nuisance problems. Sound familiar? Yet what happens when the agency fails to adjust purchasing processes for buying supplies like live traps or fencing? Or what happens when the agency fails to adjust travel approval processes for travel outside the precinct or county? Employees may wait unnecessarily to get approval to buy needed fencing and traps, or travel to address a nuisance wildlife issue may be delayed while waiting for burdensome travel approvals. These two misalignments in decision processes alone can result in far less than expedient agency responses to wildlife nuisance calls.

In this example, the agency failed in Blenko's point number one: identifying key decisions. This misalignment might have been corrected if the agency had used point two (changing where in the organization the decisions should happen). Perhaps decisions could have been made at the field level instead of at the agency headquarters in the accounting section. Even Blenko's point three (organizing macrostructure around values to clients) may have helped. For example, a specific work unit in the organization could be designed just to handle nuisance wildlife complaints if that was deemed so important. Certainly attention to point four could have helped by giving the level of authority to decide purchases and travel authorization to those who must do the work. The bottom line is that **all** the decision processes must be aligned with the desired results for the agency to succeed.

STRUCTURE

Structure addresses who reports to whom, and this alignment is one of the Big Six that must be gotten right for maximum effectiveness. Nobody wants two bosses. It's not uncommon in fish and wildlife agencies, however, to have a field employee reporting to someone in the field and also to someone at headquarters. Again, the main concern is that the agency's structure supports both the decision process and work process components of the Big Six. Why? Because structure, decision processes, and work processes need to be designed to implement the strategies encompassed in the methods blade of the helicopter model.

If the decision processes and the work processes are not reflected in the structure, then problems are inevitable. Blenko, et al. (2010) state "that nearly half of all corporate CEOs launch a reorganization during their first two years on the job and less than one third of those reorganizations produce any meaningful improvement." I believe that a major reason for this dismal success rate is the act of focusing solely on structure while failing to align collectively all of the Big Six components of the organization.

PEOPLE AND TRAINING

Agencies achieve the best results when they have the right employees in the right positions. As Jim Collins (2001) writes, "The right people should be on the bus and in the right seats on the bus." According to Buckingham and Coffman (1999), this is a matter of selecting people whose unique nature fits the needs of the agency rather than trying to change the people to fit what the agency needs. If the right people are hired to start with, future problems are much less likely to occur and vice versa. Chris Smith, a former state fish and wildlife agency deputy director (pers. comm.), recommends "even passing on filling a position if you don't have the right applicant. Leaving a position vacant for a couple more months while you search for better candidates is much less harmful than hiring the wrong person and having to deal with the consequences of that decision for years."

Another tool is the use of a probationary period. I've seen weak supervisors who realized someone was not right for the job, yet the supervisor lacked the courage to make the tough call to terminate the employee during the probationary period. It is important to address hiring mistakes quickly. I was once involved in hiring an administrative assistant who stated in her interview she had a great skill set. After the first few days on the job, however, it was apparent she did not possess the skills she had professed.

At the end of her first week of employment, the administrative assistant deleted and moved very important files on the office server, creating a major problem for all the staff. The next week I was involved in the firing of that person. It was important to do it as soon as the problem became apparent. To delay was not fair to the employee and surely not to the rest of the office.

Because this employee was on probation, she could be fired with none of the potential legal complications had she become a permanent employee. Of course, the employee wasn't happy about it. She complained that she had not had time to even learn the job. But it was clear that she made poor decisions and her skill set was not even close to what she had claimed in her résumé or interview. In reality, the hard decision to quickly terminate the employee was best for the organization and it helped the employee by not stringing her along in a job for which she was not equipped.

An important learning point for me was that, thereafter, I never accepted at face value a job applicant's claimed skill set. From then on, I always required applicants to demonstrate their skills as part of the application process.

Those with supervisor responsibilities in government agencies can develop a defeatist attitude toward getting the right people into the right jobs. They may view employees as "headless nails" in that once they are in a position, they can't be removed. Granted, it's a challenge, but it's well worth the effort to use the human resource processes that are in place to remove people that are wrong for their job. Retaining people who are not effective, and who become obstacles for getting the job done well, cripples an agency and destroys employee morale.

TERMINATING EMPLOYEES

Removing ineffective employees usually involves creating a performance improvement plan with the employee, then meeting with the employee regularly (I recommend weekly) to assess improvements in performance or lack thereof. It is important to document in writing the regular meetings to assess improvements. Have the employee sign each written document. The result of this process can be eventual work improvement, or at least a clear paper trail leading to successful termination of the employee. For specific agency requirements regarding termination of an employee, contact your human resources staff.

I've found that when supervisors avoid the important task of removing an underperforming employee, that avoidance is enabled by the supervisor's boss failing to hold the **supervisor** accountable. Firing is a most important supervisory task. Without it, the ultimate result is agency mediocrity and lack of motivation for good employees to do an excellent job.

It's a matter of accountability down the chain of command, from the director holding his or her staff accountable for dealing with personnel issues, to the staff holding those below them with supervisory responsibilities accountable, and so on. It starts at the top. There's often fear of lawsuits from fired employees and the cost and time of having to deal with them. This is a real possibility, but that's why supervisors need to follow all the protocols and documentation required before firing someone. It is not a reason to avoid letting undesirable employees go.

Unfounded lawsuits from fired employees are best dealt with by **support from the agency hierarchy.** Agency lawyers may recommend settling out of court to prevent drawn out and costly court battles. In some cases, this is an option for saving time and money, but the downside is that it makes the agency and the supervisor appear at fault! This can be damaging to the careers of those supervisors, and basically it's the agency caving to the fired employee. Caving by agency upper administration makes it harder for other supervisors to then take on the task of firing an employee in the future. Caving sends supervisors the message that the agency will not support their action (no matter how correct). Consider this organizational cost when contemplating saving time and money by settling out of court over the termination of an employee.

Max Peterson (pers. comm.), a former Chief of the U.S. Forest Service, once made the analogy that "Organizations are like trees—they die from the top down." If there are problems with personnel in the wrong jobs or performing poorly, look first in upper level administration to see if they are holding their direct reports accountable. I am familiar with cases in fish and wildlife agencies where those working immediately for the director have gone years without any performance review. Upper administration often seems to believe that because their direct reports are "good people," it is unnecessary to take the time from busy and chaotic schedules to conduct performance reviews. Avoiding this step in ensuring accountability at the top sends the wrong signal down through the ranks.

No one wants to deal with the tangled web of labor unions, human resources, and rules and policies that are "the epoxy that greases the wheels of government" (Borden 1972). In most cases it's much easier for anyone to live with their current situation than make real change. They have to ask themselves two questions: *How committed am I to really making a difference*? *Am I satisfied with taking the easy way out and doing nothing*?

Sometimes a person may not be able to perform a job well, but might be able to if they had the proper training and skill set. This situation is easier to address than the poor performer who is neither motivated nor capable of performing well despite proper training. After all, it is relatively easy to provide training if management supports it. However, the rush of day-to-day work, lack of funds for training, reluctance to spare the person from their job to take training, and many other excuses often leads agencies to provide it only minimally or neglect training altogether.

In my work, I see a variety of examples of the consequences of neglected training. For instance, public agencies often go through periods where there's an emphasis on public involvement. But their field staff may have little experience with the proper methods for effectively engaging publics. The field staff may be told to *go forth and hold public meetings*. It's like giving an untrained person a chainsaw and asking them to cut a cord of wood. The potential for damage is great, yet I see it regularly. The employee typically suffers a disastrous public meeting or two and then tries to avoid them like the plague the rest of his or her career. The same results apply to teams where there is no training or mentoring on how to engender teamwork or manage teams. There are many other examples similar to these two. The point is that the right person with the right training is critical to effective organizational operation.

Another common problem that affects training stems from modeling behaviors of the director and his or her top management team. How many times has a director stepped out of a training session for employees because she or he had something more important to do? Or even worse, the director never takes a training course himself or herself. Agency directors, like most staff, have busy schedules, which makes it hard to pause for a training session. While the workloads may be heavy, not taking training is foolish. Like Stephen Covey (1989) once said, "It's like driving really fast to get to an event and not wanting to take time to stop for gas." The messages sent by upper administrators through their lack of attendance at training are: *Training is not as important as your daily work, and if you are the director, or top management, then you have little left to learn.* Merely *saying* something different will not counteract such strong behavioral messages. In summary, the right people and training are critical components of the Big Six in the helicopter model's organization blade.

REWARD SYSTEMS

When reward systems are aligned to encourage the desired behaviors and results, they become a powerful component of the Big Six. Unfortunately, reward systems typically are nonexistent or at best minimal in state fish and wildlife agencies. There may be a number of excuses. One is the belief that *we cannot give monetary rewards like they do in private businesses so we cannot provide effective rewards.*

The reality is that a system of rewards is a sign of effective management at the top. Contrary to popular belief, money is not the best reward. Believing so is the result of confusing what people like with what will encourage people to work harder. Ask yourself the question: "Would I like a raise in pay?" The answer is "yes." Now ask; "If I get a raise, would I really work harder than I do now?" Most people do not work harder as a result of an increase in pay.

Recognition, a sense of belonging, and a sense of achieving something meaningful are much more powerful incentives than a few dollars weekly raise in pay or a bonus at the end of the year. If you're still skeptical, I refer you to Maslow's (1943) "Hierarchy of Needs." Volumes of research support the power of what he defines as "the higher psychological needs." Actions such as recognition in front of one's peers, a handwritten "thank you" note from the agency director for a job well done, a day off, a simple plaque—all of these are types of rewards within the grasp of the most cash-strapped agency.

These types of rewards are potentially very meaningful to deserving employees but also individually specific regarding their effectiveness with each employee. Not all people respond equally to the same type of reward. Some may bask in the recognition received in front of their peers, while others may shun the limelight. Some would prefer a day off, while others would prefer receiving a handwritten note of recognition from the director. Bottom line: it's important to tailor the reward to the recipient.

Promotions are a major reward. They speak volumes about agency values and how serious the agency is about different initiatives. Let's look at the all-too-common scenario where an agency promotes someone who fought the agency's new direction and changes every step of the way. This person gets promoted because the hiring and promotion process is not aligned with the agency's direction and values. When hiring, there's a tendency to forget all about new directions the agency has said were important. Instead, the focus goes to the most years of experience, education, and seniority. This is a major error! It sends a clear signal to all the rest of the employees. Promoting one of the people who fought most strongly against the agency's new direction says rather poignantly that the new direction is not really that important. That agency's rewards system is misaligned!

Ideally, a rewards system is carefully crafted and put in place to align perfectly with implementing the strategies to meet the constituent's needs and expectations. If you want different organizational behaviors than you are currently getting, remember the old axiom: *You get what you reward*! Still, I find that reward systems get minimal attention in state fish and wildlife agencies. Wildlife agencies rely more heavily on the "missionary-like zeal" (Kennedy 1985) of their employees for tireless effort. Those employees' commitment to preserving and managing the wildlife resources for which they are responsible is a unique, cultural characteristic in the wildlife profession that has become the default, unconsciously held expectation for a commitment to excellent performance. This reliance on zeal without a carefully aligned rewards system relegates the direction of zealous work to individual employee preferences.

So far I've been discussing positive rewards or incentives. An agency's reward system also needs to carefully use negative rewards—an absence of positive rewards, and also sanctions or reprimands. All rewards and sanctions must be aligned with the agency's direction and priorities so that everything works to facilitate, rather than block, progress. If there is no penalty for doing a poor job or for clinging stubbornly to the old methods and resisting implementation of desired changes, then there's little hope for real improvement in an agency.

Bad behaviors going unpunished and good behaviors going unrewarded are a recipe for failure in agency improvement! But I see it a lot. Many top agency administrators are unsure how to handle poor behaviors or they lack the courage to do so. They resign themselves to the fact that change is almost impossible, while at the same time their employees complain about lack of accountability from their peers. Employee initiative is further eroded by such practices as equal pay raises for all employees based upon longevity, ignoring differences in performance. Don't let these practices usurp using a well-aligned system of rewards.

INFORMATION PROCESSES
When assessing an agency's information processes, the question to ask is: Do *the right people get the information they need when they need it, and in the way they need it?* I especially remember one fish and wildlife agency that had a broken information system. The agency's conservation law enforcement officers regularly found out about regulation changes by reading about them in the newspaper! Talk about a major breakdown of the information system, not to mention a breakdown in trust.

When publics hear about regulations before those who are supposed to enforce the regulations, it reduces credibility for the agency in general and for enforcement officers in particular. An information audit may be helpful for an agency. I recommend at least developing a flow chart to illustrate the flow of information and who is responsible and authorized for passing information up and down the chain of command. Look for information gaps and where information is being stalled.

During one agency review conducted by the MAT Team, we found that a high-level manager was blocking information coming up from the ranks. He was also blocking information going down to the field. This senior manager illustrated a concept described by Gardener (1990), who wrote, "One of the most valid forms of power is the capacity to command the channels of communication."

This particular agency administrator's communications process created havoc for staff and uncertainty for upper-level administration. The senior manager could spin events in whatever way he desired by blocking information. Fortunately, the agency removed this person from his position after what was occurring came to light in the review. The agency then created a new position for the senior manager where his failings in communication could do less harm.

Most failures of information processes are due to a lack of follow-through in passing along the information, or poor attention to information received, rather than manipulation or malice. It's important to have accountability for passing along appropriate information, but it's also important to refrain from creating information overload. This requires a balance of making sure people have the information they need when they need it, not just doing an information dump.

One fish and wildlife agency used a bright red envelope to pass along extremely high priority information so that it wouldn't get lost in the avalanche of daily minutia. This color-coding idea can also be applied to electronic communications as well.

Another agency asked its law enforcement staff to develop a protocol for information delivery up and down the chain of command, and then held everyone accountable for using it. Whatever the process, it needs to be aligned to ensure those in need of information receive it in the appropriate format and in time to meet their needs.

WORK PROCESSES
Work processes must also be aligned with desired results just like the other five organizational pieces. It's easier to think of work processes as bundles of tasks used to carry out a "work project." Work projects and the inherent processes for carrying them out must be correctly aligned with the overall desired results. For example, if public participation and buy-in are desired agency outcomes, and the regulation-setting process for hunting and fishing regulations typically excludes certain constituent groups, then the work process for regulation setting is out of alignment with the desired agency results.

Another type of work process misalignment became apparent when I worked for the Montana Department of Fish, Wildlife & Parks. The incident entailed the agency's process for releasing grizzly bears from culvert traps. The desired outcomes were release of trapped bears where both the bears and employees were safe. This work process in use required someone to climb up on the top of the trap and raise the gate to release the bear. The trap was in the bed of a pickup, and when the bear exited the trap onto the ground, the truck was to drive away with the person on top of the trap transported to safety.

In this case, the work process was not in good alignment with the desired results. A game warden, Lou Kiss, was following procedures by standing on top of a trap, which was in the bed of a pickup truck. He was releasing a bear near Kalispell, Montana. When the 500-pound boar grizzly came out of the trap, Lou turned to the driver and said, "Go!" But the driver failed to respond immediately in driving away.

The bear, heard Lou say "Go," turned, and spotted Lou perched on top of the trap. The bear stood on his hind legs and placed his front paws on the end of the culvert trap that was sticking out of the truck bed. Five hundred pounds of pressure on the end of the trap protruding out of the truck bed tilted the trap, catapulting Lou off and right onto the bear's back! Fortunately, Lou had his service revolver and was lucky enough to dispatch the bear. Lou suffered only a cracked femur where the bear had latched onto his leg. The work process for releasing bears had to be changed! In most work processes, what needs changing is not as obvious and certainly not as dramatic.

One more example of misaligned work processes involved a fish and wildlife agency's process for purchasing land. The desired result was to purchase from willing sellers land that would make good wildlife habitat. Landowners desiring to sell to that agency usually wanted to complete a sale within a couple of months. However, the agency's process for purchasing land took a minimum of eighteen months to complete. Clearly, the process for this type of work was misaligned. Many land deals were lost due to the agency's inability to buy land in an expedient manner. There was a happy ending in this instance. After several land purchases fell through, that agency revised its requirements and worked with the other oversight agencies in their state government to get the land purchase process shortened to just six months.

As you may have noticed, the first three blades of the *Helicopter Model* (*Identify Constituents and Their Needs, Decide Purposes,* and *Select Methods/ Strategies*) are typical steps in developing an agency's strategic plan. However, strategic plans are greatly under-implemented and often have no impact on the direction of the agency or its work. A main reason for this failure is that the necessary changes are never made in the agency's

Big Six of their organization blade to realign the agency to implement the proposed strategic direction.

A pervasive belief is that stating direction, via a written plan and providing copies to staff, will make change happen! Such naiveté shows a lack of understanding regarding alignment of the Big Six organizational pieces and the impacts on an agency. It's much easier to just write a lofty plan with good sounding goals and solid objectives. If the process stops there, it means no one has to do anything different than they've done before. Therefore, nothing changes, regardless of what may be written in the plan.

There is good news—all of the agency's Big Six components in the organization blade do not necessarily have to be realigned to achieve new or different results. My recommendation is to review the alignments the agency currently has and identify which ones (if any) of the Big Six are misaligned and impeding the achievement of new or different results. If there are multiple misalignments, then choose the one or two that will produce the greatest leverage for achieving the agency goals. Focus on them first.

Make no mistake, realigning one or more of the Big Six will mean changing some things in the agency and there will be resistance. As John Kotter (1996) says in his book *Leading Change*, "People do not resist change. They resist loss." People can embrace change if the motivation is great enough. As Linsky (pers. comm.) says, "I have yet to meet the person that failed to turn in a winning mega-million lottery ticket because it would change their life!" Unfortunately, when things in an organization change, there is loss for at least some. This loss may mean loss of familiarity with how things are done, loss of power and stature, loss of money and people in one part of the organization versus another, etc. These are the real causes for resistance.

There are entire books about carrying out organizational change. I've condensed some of this information into the chapter in this book entitled *Changing the Organization*. Early on, it is important to recognize that some people will experience loss with change. Acknowledge it and attempt to help those suffering the loss. Help those losing their jobs with retooling their skills or searching for new jobs. If some are likely to lose status or resources in their work section, then acknowledge it and help them to deal with these losses. Ignoring the losses makes things worse for those affected. Others in the agency watch closely how the organization treats those who suffer losses. This is a major factor in what kind of morale the agency's remaining employees will have after changes in the Big Six.

The organization blade has six big pieces: 1) the right structure, 2) the right people and training, 3) the right rewards, 4) the right information processes, 5) the right decision processes and 6) the right work processes. All of these must be aligned with the agency's direction and priorities to get the desired agency results. Is your agency getting the results it desires? To paraphrase the organization design expert, Arthur W. Jones, "Currently, your agency is perfectly aligned to get the results it's getting!"

5. The Actions Blade

The *actions* helicopter blade refers to the actual behaviors people exhibit at work. The idea is that if you can influence employee actions, then you can influence the agency direction and the products and services it provides! All the previous blades of the Helicopter Model lead up to influencing employee's actions. Aligning the agency's Big Six pieces in the organizing blade is instrumental in driving employees' actions. People respond to the system in which they work. If you put smart people in stupid systems, you get stupid behaviors. Often the explanations and solutions to poor work behaviors lay hidden in the systems, processes, and structures that are in place.

I find that either one or a combination of four factors can explain the actions of employees. If actions are not what is desired, then the employee(s)

1. Are not clear on expectations of them,
2. Do not have the resources needed,
3. Do not know how to do the job correctly, or
4. Are not motivated to do the job as desired.

Clarifying expectations is a matter of clearly communicating the desired results while providing sideboards for actions and the authority to take actions to accomplish the work. It is not a matter of dictating **how** the work should be done but **what** is to be achieved! U.S. Army General George S. Patton is credited with the quote that sums it up best: "Never tell people how to do things. Tell them what to do and they will surprise you with their ingenuity" (Patton 2015).

Providing resources is part of the alignment of decision and budgeting processes previously discussed. Training on how to do the job correctly has been discussed as part of *getting the right people on the bus and in the right seats*. Aligning the processes, systems, and structures to provide this is part of the previous discussion about the Big Six. The most difficult factor to overcome in employee actions is that of motivation. How is the agency's reward system aligned? Does the agency reward poor behavior or not sanction misbehaviors? Taking a strong look at misalignments in the reward systems is key to solving motivation problems.

Motivation is also influenced by another factor, that is, the employees and their views and paradigms related to their work. This will be discussed later as the "hub" of the Helicopter Model.

6. *The Results Blade*

This blade of the Helicopter Model represents the end products of the agency—those goods and services that the agency provides for its constituents. What the majority of agency employees do at work the bulk of their time (their actions) produces these results. Assessment of the agency's performance in meeting constituents' needs and expectations is done by comparing the results the agency produces with the first blade of the Helicopter Model—*constituent needs and expectations*. If the organization's results do not meet constituents' needs and expectations, then it's time to search through the previously described blades of the model for misalignments between what the agency *desires* to produce and what it is *actually achieving*.

Agency Culture—the Hub of the Helicopter Model

The "hub" of the Helicopter Model represents the agency culture. It refers to the paradigms, values, attitudes, and beliefs of employees, shared collectively and mostly subconsciously. Edgar Schein (1992) defines culture as "A pattern of shared basic assumptions that the group learned as it solved its problems of external adaptation and internal integration, that has worked well enough to be considered valid and, therefore, to be taught to new members as the correct way to perceive, think, and feel in relation to those problems." In short, your agency's culture greatly influences the way people behave at work most of the time. Thus, your agency's culture greatly affects the **results** achieved by your agency.

John Kotter (1996) believes that culture is powerful for three primary reasons:

1. *Because individuals are selected and indoctrinated so well.*
2. *Because the culture exerts itself through the actions of hundreds or thousands of people.*
3. *Because all of this happens without much conscious intent and thus is difficult to challenge or even discuss.*

So what are you to do if realignment of the agency culture is necessary for the agency to achieve new, desirable results? Tackling the culture first is probably unwise and will likely engender massive resistance. John Kotter (1996) lists eight steps for leading change in organizations (see the chapter in this book entitled *Changing the Organization*). He lists changing the culture last, not first, in his eight-stage process. This differs from what many popular writers on the subject have advocated. I believe Kotter's approach is a very important departure from previous conventional thought because he advises:

"Culture changes only after you have successfully altered people's actions, after the new behavior produces some group benefit for a period of time, and after people see the connection between the new actions and the performance improvement."

The bottom line is to strive to change behaviors first through alignments in the reward systems and other parts of the *organization* blade. A word of caution here: any agency's culture has developed over years of certain kinds of experiences. It usually takes at least several years of different kinds of experiences to change an entrenched or "anchored" culture. The key is to keep attending to and nurturing the new change while at the same time pruning back the old ways in order to prevent them from creeping back into the agency. It requires constant vigilance over time. The basic question to ask is: A*re you and your top management ready to make this commitment?*

Applying the Helicopter Model to Design a New Program, Work Unit, or Agency

Now that I have discussed the different components of the Helicopter Model and their interrelatedness, let's look at applying the model. The model can be used to **design** a new program or work unit within an agency or to **design** a complete, new agency. The design application of the model starts at the helicopter blade labeled C*onstituents* and moves **clockwise** around the model in sequence.

For example, begin by answering the question: W*ho are our constituents and what are their needs and expectations from this program, work unit, or agency?* Answering that question then leads to the second helicopter blade labeled P*urpose.* Here, answer the question: K*nowing what the constituents need/want, what must be the purpose or mission for this program, work unit, or agency?* Once you've answered the purpose question, then move to the next blade labeled M*ethods* (often known as strategies). At this point the purpose is already decided, so the subsequent decision is: W*hat will be the methods/strategies that best enable fulfillment of purpose?* Answering that question allows us to progress to the next blade—O*rganization.*

Having decided the methods and strategies to be used allows posing the question: W*hat is the most effective way to organize processes, systems, and structure* (think Big Six components) *to best use the methods and strategies to achieve the defined purpose, thus meeting the constituents' needs and expectations?*

After deciding on the desired organization for the program, work unit, or agency, move to the next blade—A*ctions.* At this point, consider: G*iven the way we organized, what actions (kinds of work efforts performed) by employees can be expected to best implement the chosen organizational processes, systems, and structure?* Note that if the Organization blade is aligned to implement specific methods and strategies, then those strategies will be carried out to meet the desired purpose.

Next, advance from Actions to the R*esults* blade and pose the question: W*hat results can be expected from employee actions?* Complete the circle

The Design Process

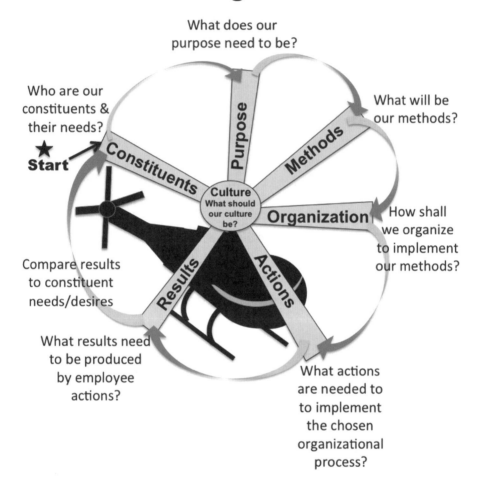

What does our
purpose need to be?

Who are our
constituents &
their needs?

★
Start

Constituents

Purpose

Methods

What will be
our methods?

Culture
What should
our culture
be?

Organization

How shall
we organize
to implement
our methods?

Compare results
to constituent
needs/desires

Results

Actions

What results need
to be produced
by employee
actions?

What actions
are needed to
to implement
the chosen
organizational
process?

around the helicopter blades, then return to the *Constituents* blade and compare expected results with the constituents' defined needs and expectations. A match is sought between results and needs/expectations. Last, focus on the hub of the Helicopter Model and answer the question: *What culture is needed to best produce the desired results?*

Using the Helicopter Model in this clockwise fashion takes you through a process of answering a series of interconnected questions in order to most effectively design a new program, work unit, or entire agency.

Applying the Helicopter Model to Diagnose Agency Performance Problems

The Helicopter Model also is very useful for **diagnosing** the failure of individual programs, work units, or agencies to sufficiently meet constituent needs and expectations. Diagnosis is the most common use of the Helicopter Model. Again, you start at the *Constituents* blade in order to use the model for diagnosis. The difference from the designing process is that the diagnosis process requires progressing around the model in a **counterclockwise** fashion.

Starting with the *Constituents* blade, you ask the questions: A*re we trying to serve the right constituents, and have we correctly identified their needs and expectations*? Next, progress to the Results blade, and ask: A*re there any gaps between what constituents need or expect and the results produced by the program, work unit, or agency*? If the answer is *no*, then there are no issues with the program, work unit, or agency.

Few things are perfect, however, and if gaps are identified, then the next step is to ask: W*hat results is the agency getting or failing to get that are causing the gaps*? The next question is: **Why** *is the agency getting those results*? Obviously, what employees do at work—their *actions*—is what produces the results. This leads to the next blade—*Actions*. Here you ask: W*hat actions are employees doing or not doing that produce insufficient or incorrect results*? The next question is: **Why** *are employees doing those actions to perform their work*? Since actions taken by employees are usually influenced greatly by how the agency organizes its Big Six components, you move to the *Organization* blade. Ask: W*hat about the way the agency is organized and aligned causes undesired employee actions*? Follow that question with: **Why** *have we chosen to organize that way*?

Since agencies are organized to best carry out chosen methods and strategies, move to the *Methods/strategies* blade. At this point ask: A*re our current methods/strategies contributing to poor organization choices or resulting in poor employee actions and thus, getting poor results*? If the answer is yes, then ask: **Why** *are we using these methods/strategies*?

Since methods and strategies are chosen in order to implement a specific purpose or mission, move to the *Purpose* blade. Ask: I*s the agency's purpose/mission still valid for the agency to meet its constituents'*

The Diagnosis Process

Is our purpose still valid to meet our constituents' needs?

Are we serving the "right" constituents and have we correctly identified their needs?

Why

Why

Are our methods contributing to poor organization choices or undesired actions?

Start →

Constituents

Purpose

Methods

Organization

Why

Culture Is our culture causing poor results

Why are we organized in a way that may be resulting in undesired employee actions?

Compare results to constituent needs/desires. Identify gaps.

Results

Actions

Why

What results are causing the gaps?

Why

Why are employees using actions that produce insufficient or incorrect results?

needs/expectations? Next ask: **Why** *has this purpose been chosen*? Since purpose is established to meet specific constituents' need/expectations, move to the *Constituents* blade and ask: **Why** *have we chosen to serve these constituents and **why** has the agency decided to identify their needs/expectations as it has*? In other words, is the agency trying to serve the *right* constituents and has it correctly identified their needs and expectations? The answers derived using this counterclockwise approach should provide a complete picture of why there is a gap between constituent needs/expectations and the agency results produced. If the picture is still incomplete or unclear, then focus next on the hub of the helicopter. The culture of the program employees, work unit employees, or agency employees may be out of alignment with the desired results. Changes in culture may be necessary in order to achieve the desired results—and that's a topic I'll save for its own discussion in the chapter *Changing the Organization*.

An example of culture misalignment occurred when one fish and wildlife agency had some employees with a cultural bias against hunting outfitters. The employees believed that no one should be allowed to make an income off the public resource of wildlife. The agency's "desired result" was to achieve involvement and buy-in from all constituents when setting hunting regulations. It seems that an employee in one geographic area of the state, who had a bias against outfitters, excluded these outfitters from the hunting regulation setting process. The result was upset outfitter constituents. The agency had to address this cultural bias of its employees in order to generate the actions necessary to produce the desired results of involvement and buy-in from all constituents.

Typically, asking all the questions as one proceeds counterclockwise around the Helicopter Model reveals a number of areas for improvement. Don't be overwhelmed if there seem to be a lot of things that need changing. As mentioned earlier, I have found that the best approach is to choose **one or two things** that will produce the greatest leverage for improving and then working to change those things first. Those items not addressed in this first change effort can be addressed later in sequence depending on their levels of importance.

In summary, proceeding around the model in a counterclockwise fashion allows you to ask the right questions in the right order to diagnose problems and to distinguish between root causes and symptoms. The process takes into account the influences of each of the model's blades on the program, work unit, or agency in question. It also allows you to take into account the interactions between each of the helicopter's blades.

Randomly choosing one part of the agency for change is akin to *tinkering*. It is an oversimplified yet common approach to dealing with brushfire issues, and it often has unexpected negative consequences even though intentions may be admirable. It is much more effective to consider all the parts of the agency and their interrelatedness before choosing ways to bring about change.

A narrow, *tinkering* type of approach is typical of those who overestimate their ability to force change on an agency. Even the agency's top authority figure will find little long-term success trying to bring about change coercively. For example, one fish and wildlife agency had a director (I'll call him Jim) appointed by the state's governor. Jim sought to make major changes in the agency using very coercive means during his four-year term of office. He moved many people in the agency, forced out several top-management staff, and changed the agency structure for what many believed were personal reasons, not professional ones. These autocratic decisions by Jim may have been well intended, but they resulted in anger, resentment, and lack of trust between the director and employees, and they drove many good employees out of the agency.

At the end of Jim's term, a previous agency director (I'll call him Hal) was reappointed to the director position. Hal was well liked and had a history of doing a good job as a top authority figure. Interestingly, I spoke with one of the agency's management team members within a few months after Hal was appointed. I was told, "It's amazing how quickly the agency and its employees abandoned the changes Jim had done his utmost to mandate."

This story illustrates the point that authority figures such as agency directors can move people around geographically and structurally, and mandate many changes, but real, lasting change in behaviors and agency results are not achieved this way. Such an approach commonly engenders fear, work avoidance, and general agency torpor. Understanding all the components in the Helicopter Model and how they relate to each other is a better alternative. It enables wise choices about which components will provide the greatest leverage for change and how changing one component will affect other components. Remember, a fish and wildlife agency is a lot like an ecosystem. When one component changes in any way, the other components will be affected.

At the beginning of this chapter, I stated that there are political as well as practical challenges to running an agency. Political concerns are a natural, inescapable part of our professional landscape. They are not all good or all bad, but they cannot be ignored. Interestingly, I see that politics often does not have effective agency management as its first priority. Osborn and Gaebler (1992) alluded to this concept when they said, "...the ultimate test in government is not performance, but reelection." While reappointment or reelection is important, doing a great job leading and managing an effective agency is also very important! The nation's wildlife resources depend on it and the Helicopter Model approach can help.

Summary

Recognizing patterns of interaction among the different parts of an agency is critical to effectively leading and managing an agency. The Helicopter Model identifies seven major parts of an organization that must be synchronized for maximum effectiveness. These are the seven blades of the model:

- **Constituents:** Deciding who will be served and how much and discerning their needs/expectations from our agency. This is a heavily value-laden decision and not an easy one to make.

- **Purpose:** Basing the agency's purpose on the decisions in the first blade.

- **Methods:** Choosing the best methods/strategies to achieve the purpose defined in the second blade. This often means changing some old methods/strategies—always guaranteed to create resistance.

- **Organization:** Aligning the organization to most effectively implement the methods and strategies selected in the third blade. This includes arranging the Big Six organizational components to function supportively each enhancing the other. The Big Six are:
  1. The right **decision processes,**
  2. The right **structure,**
  3. The right **people and training,**
  4. The right **rewards system,**
  5. The right **information processes,**
  6. The right **work processes.**

- **Actions:** The actions of employees—what most people do at work most of the time—is what determines the end products and services of the agency. Employee actions are mostly driven by the organization of the Big Six. Realizing this and aligning the organization to achieve the desired actions is critical to success.

- **Results:** The end products and services delivered are usually determined in large part by the decisions made in the previous five helicopter blades. Results should be compared with the first blade (constituents) to see if the needs/expectations of constituents are being met.

- **Culture:** The culture—paradigms, values, and beliefs of employees—is perhaps the primary influence on employee actions. If the other blades are aligned but there is still a gap between what constituents need/expect, then the hub of culture may need to be addressed to achieve agency effectiveness. Changing agency culture is a difficult but not impossible task.

The Helicopter Model can be used as a tool at various levels within an agency. It can be used for designing a new program, work unit, or whole agency by starting at the Constituent blade and addressing questions for each blade while moving clockwise around the model. The model also can be used for a diagnosis of the agency by starting at the Constituent blade and following the model counterclockwise, asking "why" at each blade.

This chapter's helicopter view of an agency from above provides the means to design agency components and to diagnose agency problems. However, there is another component of agency leadership and management that the model does not address and that is the commissions many agencies answer to. Commissions can be a great asset or an albatross for an agency. The next chapter addresses successful agency-commission relationships based upon sound policies.

Literature Cited

Blenko, M. W., M. C. Mankins, and P. Rogers. 2010. "The Decision-Driven Organization." *Harvard Business Review*. Boston, MA.

Boren, James H. 1972. *When in Doubt, Mumble: A Bureaucrat's Handbook*. Van Nostrad Reinhold Co. New York, NY. 172 pp.

Buckingham, Marcus and Curt Coffman. 1999. *First, Break All the Rules— What the World's Greatest Managers Do Differently*. Simon and Schuster, New York, NY. 261 pp.

Collins, Jim. 2001. *Good to Great*. Harper Collins Publishers, Inc. New York, NY. 300 pp.

Covey, Stephen R. 1989. *Seven Habits of Highly Effective People*. Simon and Schuster, Inc. New York, NY. 358 pp.

FranklinCovey Company. 1995. *The Four Roles of Leadership*. Workshop booklet. FranklinCovey Company. Salt Lake City, UT.

Gardner, J. W. 1990. *John Gardner on Leadership*. The Free Press. New York, NY. 220 pp.

Geist, V., S. P. Mahoney, and J.F. Organ. 2001. "Why Hunting has Defined the North American Model of Wildlife Conservation." Transactions North American Wildlife and Natural Resources Conference. 66: 175-185.

Gigliotti, L. M., D. L. Shroufe, and S. Gurtin. 1009. "The Changing Culture of Wildlife Management." In *Wildlife and Society: The Science of Human Dimensions*. M. J. Manfredo, J. J. Vaske, P. J. Brown, D. J. Decker, and E. A. Duke (Eds.), Island Press. Washington, D.C.

Kennedy, J. J. (1985). "Viewing Wildlife Managers as a Unique Professional Culture." *The Wildlife Society Bulletin*. 13 (4), pp. 571-579.

Kotter, John. 1996. *Leading Change*. Harvard Business School Press. Boston, MA. 187 pp.

Maslow, Abraham. 1943. "A Theory of Human Motivation." *Psychological Review*. 50(4). pp. 370-396.

Mourier, Pierre and Martin Smith. 2001. *Conquering Organizational Change*. CEP Press. Atlanta, GA. 212 pp.

Osborne, David, and Ted Gaebler. 1992. *Reinventing Government*. Addison-Wesley Publishing Inc. New York, NY. 405 pp.

Patton, George S. 2015. http://www.generalpatton.com/quotes/index3.html

Schein, Edgar H. 1992. *Organizational Culture and Leadership*. Jossey-Bass. San Francisco, CA. 418 pp.

U.S. Dept. of the Interior, Fish and Wildlife Service, and U.S. Dept. Commerce, U.S. Census Bureau. 2006. *National Survey of Fishing, Hunting, and Wildlife-Associated Recreation*. 164 pp.

CHAPTER THREE

Commissions and
Agency Governance

It was a bright summer day in the Northeast. Three of us sat in a small meeting room adjacent to the director's office. Two of us from the Association of Fish & Wildlife Agencies Management Assistance Team were discussing a comprehensive agency review with the deputy director while the director was meeting with the agency's commission chairman in the next room. A wooden door separated the two rooms.

As we continued our discussion with the deputy director, we could hear the commission chairman's voice in the next room rising in volume. He apparently didn't know we were next door unavoidably eavesdropping on his harangue. As the chairman's voice grew louder we could feel the tension and hear the downright bullying. The chairman began to threaten the director, using foul language. The rage and vehemence of the chairman was palpable. Amazingly, the director took the verbal abuse calmly, even as his commission chairman stormed out of the office and slammed the door.

When we looked at the deputy director, he averted his eyes, obviously embarrassed by the chairman's bullying behavior. It was an awkward moment for us but nothing compared to what that director had just gone through. The deputy director apologized for the incident and everyone tried to ignore the whole episode.

As a colleague has observed, "The commission form of governance is the very best form of government when the commission and director understand their respective roles in the process to work together for a mutual cause. However, when that doesn't occur, the commission form of governance can be the worst form of government" (John Arway pers. comm.) It's a fact that individual commissioners, as well as whole commissions, can pose significant difficulties for agency directors. The reverse is also true—agency directors can be trouble for progressive commissioners. Fortunately, both can be great assets to one another as well. The question is *how*?

During my years working with many commissions across the nation, I've seen a wide range of behavior, from good to bad. The problem for many agency directors is how to ensure an effective working relationship with their commission instead of evoking anger, resentment, lack of trust, and separate agendas on both sides of the relationship. One answer is found in commissions identifying and articulating a **system** of governance that delineates individual and group authority levels, procedural norms, and clear, distinct roles for the commission, the director, and agency staff. This chapter examines the distinct roles of directors and commissions and recommends a set of principles and strategies for a positive system of governance.

The Governance System

Many commissions operate based on cobbled together bits of relevant statutes, Roberts Rules of Order, and historical protocols rather than from any well-thought-out governance design. Lack of a well-structured system of governance is one of the main causes for dysfunction in today's fish and wildlife commissions.

You've probably heard it asked before, W*hy do smart people often do seemingly stupid things when they act as a group*? Well, it's no different with commissions. For optimum commission effectiveness, its members must first do the good foundational work of developing their protocols and processes and other "rules of the road" for how they will carry on their commission work. Sure, most commissions follow their state's statutory requirements and parliamentary procedures (usually Roberts' Rules of

Order). These are reasonable first steps but woefully insufficient solutions for the full spectrum of a contemporary commission's job.

The bullying overheard in the director's office described at the beginning of this chapter most likely would not have occurred if that commission and agency had a working system of governance. That anecdote is just one example of how a single commissioner can mistakenly assume he or she has personal and separate power to give orders to the director. In fact, individual commissioners hold only one portion of the collective power of the commission as a whole.

Trust

Trust is often the first causality of poorly structured governance processes. When roles are not clearly defined and thus vary in interpretation, there is great opportunity for self-serving decisions, egocentric actions, and a breakdown of trust. Some commissioners come to the job with previous experience on **operating** boards such as school boards or conservation group boards, bringing with them the expectation that they will have a say in day-to-day operational activities. But commissions are **governing** boards. As such, they oversee strategic and policy direction. When this distinction is not made clear, trust suffers.

Also, big egos can play a major role in director-commission interactions since at least some, and often a majority, of commissioners and directors are Type A personalities. I've seen instances of commissioners who demanded the stocking of private ponds owned by the commissioner or their friends, commissioners seeking stocking of exotic wildlife on their private ranches, and commissioners shamelessly promoting regulations that benefit their personal business interests such as outfitting or decoy manufacturing.

Once broken, trust usually spirals downward. The most common response I've seen to environments of low trust is directors who "protect" themselves and their agency from commission "interference" by keeping their commissions at arms length. These directors stage manage their commission's process and pacify commissioners by doing much of the work for them and by staging meetings and events to make the commissioners still feel important.

I've found that people who serve as commissioners overall are civic-minded people who want to make a positive contribution to their community. Most commissioners are unpaid for their work, and most recognize from the beginning that serving as a commissioner won't be easy. Agency directors overall want to do a good job as well, and they know their task will be difficult. However, even well intentioned people can find themselves in low-trust environments with individuals exhibiting a myriad of uncooperative behaviors when there is no clear system of governance within which to operate. Building and maintaining trust is dependent on instituting a system of commission governance that defines clear roles and levels of authority for individual commissioners, the commission as a whole, the agency director, and agency staff. In addition, a successful system of governance requires **strict adherence** to role distinctions—how the commission, director, and agency staff operate—as well as to strict protocols for how the commission communicates with the director and staff.

Confusion over Power

Power is an elusive and intangible ingredient in commission operations. It is influenced by commission dynamics and the formation of alliances between commissioners. These alliances and dynamics can shift from issue to issue over time.

It is no wonder that confusion about distribution of power is a common problem for commissions. *Does a person appointed as a commissioner have separable and individual power because of that appointment, or does that commissioner only have shared power channeled through the collective action of the commission as a whole?* Unless this is explicitly clarified, commissioners typically assume that they have individual power. A lack of common agreement and understanding of individual commissioner authority, versus a commission's group authority, versus the agency director's authority, is the basis for much discontent and abuse of power. An example is the story at the beginning of this chapter about the commission chairman's tirade aimed at the agency director. Other examples of abuse of authority include commissioners berating agency staff in public commission meetings and commissioners demanding wildlife management actions (in one case involving the killing of raptors) that are both illegal and biologically unsupportable. On the other hand, I have also observed directors regularly "stage managing" their commission or downright manipulating them through such means as withholding information.

Fortunately, there also is a track record of successes. I've seen commissions work very well with agency directors, building trust and cooperation. These directors and their commissions have evolved understanding and trust for how they work together. When a new commissioner is appointed, the other commissioners actively bring the new member on board with their work culture, role, and level of authority. These successful commissions usually have high trust levels and a cooperative spirit. Both the commission and the director are committed to making the agency successful in providing products, services, and recreational and commercial opportunities from the agency's fisheries and wildlife management efforts. Again, the difference between success and failure amid commissions and agency directors and their staff lies in every instance with having a system of governance that clearly defines what powers belong to what positions.

Clarity of Purpose, Roles, and Authority

In addition to clarifying the powers associated with the different positions of those in the commission governance process, a well-planned system of governance spells out the commission's purpose and defines procedures for how the commission will operate effectively. John and Miriam Carver are the experts who have taken the design of this process as their career work. The Carvers have worked with many government boards and commissions as well as those from the private and non-profit sectors (Carver 1997 and J. Carver and M. Carver 1997). I present the Carvers' principles in this chapter as a positive roadmap that fish and wildlife commissions can begin using right away to improve their system of commission governance. For details on each of these principles, see the Carver Institute website (http://www.carvergovernance.com/) and several of the Carvers' books listed in the literature cited at the end of this chapter.

Responsibilities and Role Distinctions

Commissions can be likened to a corporate board of directors. The commission or board is responsible to the "owners" of the natural resources, that is, the citizens of the state. Commissioners are responsible for seeing to it that their state's natural resources are well managed and that wildlife-related recreational and commercial opportunities are provided in a way that benefits all the "owners." The users of the wildlife resources include such diverse groups as wildlife watchers, hunters, anglers, and commercial guides and fishermen. It is one way the public trust doctrine (Sax 1970) is implemented for wildlife in this country. This is similar to the way a corporate board is responsible to its owners (shareholders) to see that their corporation is managed well and provides a suitable return on investments.

The Agency Director's Five Roles

The agency director can be likened to the CEO of a corporation and has similar roles:

1. Achievement of end results produced by the agency
2. Control of day-to-day operations of the agency
3. Supervision of the agency employees
4. Ensure all means used by the agency and its employees are acceptable to the commission
5. Fiscal responsibility by conforming to a balanced budget

In well functioning governance systems it is not the commissioner or board member's role to supervise employees, be 'super staff' for the agency, or mini-directors on specific issues. Instead, the agency director or corporate CEO carries out their executive management role following commission or board direction on what end results are to be achieved. This direction is given by commissioners carrying out their role through policy setting and following the statutory rules from their elected officials. In other words, commissions define the results or 'ends' to be achieved and the director implements methods to achieve these. Sideboards are also set by the commission to define unacceptable actions that bind the director or CEO. At this high level of description, the roles seem clear and manageable, but the devil resides in the details of implementation. Let's explore the commission's roles in detail.

The Commission's Six Roles

If you really want to improve your commission then consider how it addresses the following six roles for which any fish and wildlife commission is responsible:

1. Linking the agency with the fish and wildlife "owners" (citizens of the state)
2. Defining the agency's end results to be achieved and for which citizens
3. Specifying means that are unacceptable to achieve the ends
4. Delegating responsibility for achieving specified end results to the director and assurance of director-agency performance
5. Specifying the commission–director/staff linkage
6. Specifying how the commission governs itself

Ask yourself: *Does your commission have written policies related to these six roles?* If not, there is a lot of work to do because the best tool for commissions to accomplish the above six roles is through written governing policies (more about this later).

Commission Role 1: Linking the agency with the fish and wildlife owners (citizens of the state)

Linking the agency with the "owners" of wildlife is one of the primary roles for a commission. The commission is appointed to represent **all** the publics of that state in fish and wildlife issues. This is no small task and is fraught with difficulties.

Typically, members of a fish and wildlife commission are appointed to represent specific geographical regions of the state. These commissioners have a major challenge in determining the best course of action when constituents from their geographical area desire a specific decision that would be detrimental to wildlife or to other constituents in other parts of the state. This can be particularly problematic when a meeting room is packed and the crowd is angry and vociferous about the need for "their" commissioner to decide in their favor. Ideally, commissioners vote for the greater good of the greater number of people in these situations. A commission operational policy to this effect is needed for all fish and wildlife commissions. Does your commission have such a specific **written** policy?

I have observed that, frequently, commissioners, agency staff, and sometimes, even agency directors are confused about what constituency the fish and wildlife agency serves. Some believe it is hunters and anglers because they are the license buyers and, thus, the major source of income for most state fish and wildlife agencies. Others believe it is hunters and anglers and some vocal non-consumptive users. The reality is that wildlife belongs to **all** citizens of the state! This is the overall group that fish and wildlife agencies and their commissions must serve. Failure to serve the overall public results in lack of support from the general populace and a reduction in the agency's relevancy to this overall group.

The inequities in the funding models of most fish and wildlife agencies places most of the funding burden on a small segment of the public composed mostly of hunters and anglers. In turn, the agencies and their commissions tend to focus most heavily on this small percent of the public to the exclusion of many.

A report by Duda et al. (1998) stated that there is a preponderance of research that suggests overall; few Americans are familiar with their state fish and wildlife agency. Some do not even know that there is such an agency, and those who have heard of it can rarely remember its name or explain its precise function.

Another report on the credibility and reputation of state fish and wildlife agencies (Case and Seng 1999) indicates there is a major gap in the connection of state fish and wildlife agencies with their citizens. For example, forty-three percent of Virginia citizens surveyed said there was no agency responsible for fish and wildlife management or that they "don't know" of such an agency. In Maryland, seventy-four percent of citizens did not know who was responsible for managing and protecting wildlife. Seventy-five percent of Delaware citizens knew little or nothing about their state fish and wildlife agency, and in Connecticut, fully ninety percent of citizens had never seen or heard anything from their agency.

Obviously, there is much room for commissions to improve in connecting state fish and wildlife agencies with their broader publics. It is unfair to expect a handful of part-time commissioners to accomplish this momentous task alone. It will take a concerted effort of the state agency staff as well as the commission members. Case and Seng (1999) list eight steps that could be considered as a starting place for both commissioners and staff:

1. Increase human dimension work to better understand constituents.
2. Embrace conflict and work to become more effective in mediating and resolving as well as preventing conflict.
3. Increase face-to-face communication with stakeholders.
4. Make one-on-one contact through technologies such as email, Facebook, Twitter, etc.
5. Be emotional—show you care (see Chapter Six: Emotion, Science, and Communication).
6. Make a commitment to customer service as part of the agency mission.
7. Spend more time and resources on communications and outreach.
8. Make good policies—building a good reputation begins with the commission, not a news release!

One of the most common commission concerns is that the input they do receive is disparate, with conflicting points of view. Commissioners have the unenviable task of trying to determine from all this conflicting information what the majority opinion may be. "Is the information I get as a commissioner really representative?" remains one of the central questions commissioners face. This is never more evident than in regular commission meetings that are open to the public. Many citizens take this opportunity to testify to the commission. Here again, the commission is faced with questions "Are the people attending this meeting truly representative of the general public's opinions and attitudes?" or "Is the meeting just filled with 'squeaky wheels' that represent opinions held by a minority of the public?"

I have witnessed numerous commission meetings where interest groups rented busses and transported large numbers of their group to commission meetings in order to "pack the house." The hope of these interest groups is that by having a majority of people with their point of view in the room, and with many of them testifying, that it would sway commission decisions. Often this ploy works!

Case and Seng's step one (increase human dimensions work) ties directly to this issue. State fish and wildlife agencies have become more rigorous in using human dimensions research to ensure they scientifically collect information that is truly representative of their publics' beliefs, values, and opinions. In fact, some progressive state fish and wildlife agencies employ one or more human dimension social scientists on a full-time basis. If your state is not making full use of this type of approach, then it is an obvious place for immediate improvements.

Another difficulty commissions face is evaluating a lot of input from small groups of the most interested constituents while receiving little input from the much larger groups with lower levels of interest. It is an accepted fact that satisfied constituents seldom attend commission meetings, and dissatisfied constituents are much more likely to attend. Commissioners usually meet with some of their constituents at various group gatherings, such as meetings of agricultural groups and sportsmen groups. Commissioners also get many phone calls and emails from constituents, and commissioners often are intercepted in public through chance meetings with interested individuals.

In these ways, commissioners continuously get input from their most vocal constituents. The question arises: "Just because some 'owners' do not give input, should those 'owners' needs be ignored even though they may be a much larger group than the more vocal groups?" So far, the commission actions I have observed indicate that if you don't speak up, then you will be ignored. Does this approach really meet the role of fully linking citizens with their fish and wildlife agency? The simple act of inviting specific representatives of other stakeholder groups, like garden clubs or civic groups, who do not normally interact with the commission to come to commission meetings and provide input would be one step toward addressing this issue.

Commission Role 2: Defining End Results (Ends) to be Achieved by the Agency and for Which Citizens

A commission is responsible for defining what end results the agency is to achieve and consequently what market segments, or publics, are to receive these benefits. These results are referred to as agency ends and need to be stipulated in written commission policies.

Commissions often fail here because of their history of making specific decisions on regulations and other lower-level decisions best left to staff.

State laws that were based upon poorly understood commission roles and operations usually require fish and wildlife regulation setting to be done by commissions. It all can become very confusing, and commissions quickly deteriorate into meddling in the minutia of day-to-day agency operational decisions. For example, I have seen commissions specify which waters to stock with fish and what brand of tractors the agency can purchase. Two important things get lost: 1) Any clarity of the overall big picture regarding what is best for the statewide conservation and use of natural resources, and 2) the best roles for commissioners.

Opening broad discussions of the agency's desired results poses the challenge of a commission working with the different and conflicting values and beliefs between commissioners as well as between citizens. Conflict management is necessary to deal with the consequential disagreement over these major issues. This challenge is further exacerbated by the fact that authority figures, including governors and commissioners, are expected to retain order and reduce conflict. The governor, who often appoints commissioners, almost always wants to reduce conflict, not generate more of it. Smooth-running, conflict-free government is what keeps a politician popular and ensures reelection. Thus, commissions, like most everyone else, are reluctant to bring up issues that will result in conflict. The ensuing consequence is to simply let sleeping dogs lie and continue on with business as usual. Commissions must exhibit the courage to employ step two of Case and Seng's eight steps—*embracing conflict and then managing it.*

Explicitly defining ends that the agency should produce, and for whom, is exactly the level of discussion that only a commission can address. Failure of commissions to fulfill this important role has led non-hunting and non-angling publics to question an agency's overall relevancy (Jacobsen 2008). For a large percent of the non-license buying population in many states, this question of state fish and wildlife agencies' relevancy is acute.

I frequently hear commissioners and agency staff making the comment: "We are a public agency; we serve everyone in the general public." Really? The truth of the matter is that state fish and wildlife agencies have limited resources, making it impossible for them to provide everything for everyone. The result is that not everyone gets served or gets served the same. Yet a commission ultimately represents the "owners" of the fish and wildlife resources—all citizens of the state. The commission's role is much broader than just serving the needs of consumptive users (license buyers). While funding sources and consequential restrictions on how funding can be spent have a major influence on which groups receive what goods and services, the commission role also entails making hard decisions about who gets served and how much within these restrictions.

A commission that fails to openly discuss and consciously decide on the end products and services that the agency is to produce then de facto relegates that choice to the agency staff, at least within the boundaries of funding and spending restrictions. The choices agency staff make in daily management decisions culminate into de facto broader choices for the agency's results—those all-important choices about who will get what services and opportunities, how much of these they will get, and at what cost! What happens is a series of separate decisions that may or may not be in alignment with any overall desired results. Thus, the agency's strategic direction, or lack thereof, is determined by the implicit accumulation of the staff's various values and cultures infused into daily decisions.

While it's true that many agencies develop strategic plans, those plans are usually below the level of overall strategic decisions about what services and products to produce for whom at what cost. The same de facto process described above influences these plans because people avoid addressing the agency's larger desired results. In addition, in my experience, strategic plans are usually not well implemented and have little real effect on the direction or strategies of the agency. This is largely due to the fact that, once the strategic plan is written, there is little to no consequential realignment of the supporting agency processes, systems, and structures (see the Big Six in Chapter Two, *A Model of Agency Interdependencies*).

When discussing the value-laden subject of choices between agency products and services (results), I find that commissions have little experience in doing this larger job. These kinds of discussions are difficult and scary for most commissioners. Commonly, commissions stay in their comfort zone, dealing with small decisions such as regulation setting, reviewing budgets, and land purchases. The reason the larger decisions are scary and can seem overwhelming is that these decisions deal with deeply held values and beliefs not only of the commissioners and staff but also of the state's citizens. Commissioners need to ask themselves: "Do I want to just direct agency operations, or is my time better spent determining the statewide fate of fish and wildlife resources?"

Important questions related to defining results may include:

- Which stakeholder group will get how much service from the agency?
- Are a program's benefits worth the costs?
- Should agencies be responsible for providing wildlife-watching opportunities on agency properties bought with sportspeople's dollars—on other properties? At what cost?
- Should license buyer's dollars pay for opportunities provided to non-license buying publics? (For example, whitewater rafters using fishing access sites at no cost since the sites are paid for with fishing license dollars.)
- How responsible is the agency for providing horseback riding or ATV opportunities on agency-owned lands?
- Should the commission influence timber harvest practices on agency-owned lands?

John and Miriam Carver (1997) recommend that commissions not determine the agency's end results in a vacuum when trying to fulfill that role. The Carvers recommend that this type of work involve listening to multiple stakeholder groups (publics) and asking stakeholder representatives to testify and discuss options. It's a continuous process that's constantly revisited as stakeholder groups change, as well as agency funding and other circumstances change. However, this role of defining what the agency should produce, at what cost, and for who is a crucial role and one that only commissions have the authority to perform. Sadly, it is a role into which commissions seldom venture.

Commission Role 3: Specifying Means That Are Unacceptable for Achieving the Ends

A third role of commissions is to keep the agency staff and director from using unacceptable means. Whether those means are considered too risky financially, too costly, unsafe, or even illegal, the unacceptable means need to be clearly defined in written policies crafted by the commission. I have yet to see a well-thought out set of such policies written by any commission with which I have worked in the last twenty-five years. At best, a long list of dos and don'ts are compiled, but more commonly, commissions do not address this overall or proactively. Instead, commissions wait until some action is taken that they deem unacceptable, then they pass specific policies related to that action. The result over time is a hodgepodge of dos and don'ts with no overall thought.

A second example of a commission dabbling in unacceptable actions is when a specific program or project is ready to be carried out by staff. Just then, the commission inserts itself into the process, often prescribing exactly how the program or project should be carried out. The problem is that once the commission prescribes the how, it cannot reasonably hold the agency director accountable should the effort fail. Yet it's not uncommon to see commissions inappropriately do this very thing.

A much better alternative is to have the commission describe the *what*, in other words, the desired results, and then leave it to the full-time, professional staff to decide the how. A commission controls implementation methods by **defining unacceptable behaviors proactively,** not by prescribing *how*. Policies in this category must all be statements of what is **not** acceptable; in other words, *thou shall not* types of statements.

To avoid developing executive limitations on behaviors for every project or program, successful commissions craft policies on unacceptable behaviors such that they apply to **all** situations. Policies may be broad or very specific. Examples include:

- **Broad** - *Do nothing that is financially irresponsible.*
  - o **More Specific** – *Don't spend more in any fiscal year than is taken in without commission approval.*
- **Broad** - *Do not behave in any way that is illegal or immoral.*
  - o **More Specific** – *Don't permit alcohol in agency offices.*
- **Broad** - *Do not place staff in unsafe conditions.*
  - o **More Specific** – *Don't use tractors without rollover protection bars.*

See the section *Developing Commission Policies* later in this chapter for more information about writing policies.

I acknowledge this type of policy setting is hard for a commission because it feels like the commission is releasing a great deal of control to its chief executive officer. Actually, the commission can be as control-ling as it deems necessary by the number and specificity of unacceptable methods it includes in policy statements. This takes us back again to the central importance of trust. If a commission has high trust of the chief ex-ecutive office, then the commission will probably make fewer and broader policies. If not, then the commission can pen a greater number of more specific policies limiting the chief executive officer's methods.

Often, when commissioners are considering adopting a process of gov-ernance by policies, they fear that they would have little to do other than making a few policies. They refer to their current preoccupation with such activities as setting numerous regulations, reviewing budgets, and ap-proving land purchases. However, confronting the thorny problem of de-sired results and how much for whom is no small task. In fact, the results policies will be a constant struggle for commissions as they continue to develop and modify them. Even after dealing with results and the much easier executive limitations policies on operational means, there is plen-ty to be done by a commission.

Commission Role 4: Delegating Responsibility for Achieving Specified Results to the Director and Assurance of Director-Agency Performance

Once the commission has defined the desired results, the commission must then delegate achievement of them to the agency CEO or execu-tive director. This is critical since the director is a full-time employee with hundreds of other full-time employees to carry out accomplish-ment of the agency results, while commissioners are part-time workers. Unfortunately, commissioners sometimes see their role as "helping" to conduct staff work or being super staff for the agency, or worse, as mini-agency directors for the issue(s) of particular interest to them.

The commission delegates the work **through** the agency director! Not only is it confusing when commissions attempt to carry out or assign staff work, it's actually a misuse of authority better spent on defining desired results, operational means limits, and other policy matters for the director.

After assigning responsibility to the agency director to achieve spe-cific desired results, the next job is for the commission to determine how to check that the results were actually achieved within the means parameters. This is done not by directly overseeing staff but rather by **requiring monitoring reports** from the agency director. For example, if a desired result is the production of x number of days of deer hunting for y number of license buyers per year at a cost similar to adjoining states, then a monitoring report should be requested from the agency director to that effect. The commission then decides if the director was in compliance. Of course, monitoring reports would be requested for different programs at different times throughout the year.

The director of the Pennsylvania Fish and Boat Commission relates that he finds the best way to measure progress is through quarterly reporting at commission meetings about how he and his staff are meeting the goals and objectives contained in the agency's strategic plan (John Arway pers. comm.). By requiring monitoring reports of some type, the commission can effectively do its job of defining the desired results to be achieved, monitoring accomplishments, and ensuring no unacceptable means are used while the commission remains out of day-to-day operations. It's a matter of having the commission's "hands" **on** the agency but not **in** the agency. Most importantly, there are no surprises from either the commission or the director.

It is common for me to get calls at my office where one or more commissioners asks for guidance on how to go about conducting a formal evaluation of the agency director. The most common problems are that the commission has not specified the results the director was to have achieved by managing the agency nor the means to be avoided! Many commissions trust the director to "do the right thing." These commissioners are trying to evaluate their director using undefined expectations. Problems soon occur when the director's interpretation of "the right thing" differs from what the commissioners were expecting. But wait, it gets worse. I have seen instances when unspecified expectations differ among the commissioners. Monitoring and holding the agency director accountable is much easier when the commission has an agreed-upon set of policies that specify the results the director is to achieve and means to be avoided. Without this, it is futile for commissions to evaluate directors.

There are two other roles effective commissions fulfill through development of policies. The first is setting policies on commission linkage to agency staff and to the agency director. These policies define communication processes for giving direction as well as information exchange. The second commission role is developing policies on commission self-governance. These policies define the rules for operation of the commission **itself** and expectations for individual commissioner behavior. These are **not** operational policies for the agency staff.

Commission Role 5: Defining Commission–Director/Staff Linkage

I've found that commission–director/staff linkage policies must be clearly defined or most transgressions occur in this area. For example, I have seen commissioners directing staff who report to the agency director, or individual commissioners requesting that the director take action on specific issues without other commissioner's agreement or even knowledge. Obviously these situations make the director's job and individual staff members' jobs untenable, and they impair the commissioners' ability to work together, resulting in declining trust levels.

How should commission–director/staff linkage policies work? Here are some suggestions:

- The commission delegates **only** to the agency director and holds him or her accountable. The director further delegates to staff. Commissioners do not direct staff; they work only with the director, assigning work to him or her only.
- Commissioners should be able to ask any staff member for **information** and vice versa. Open communication between staff and commissioners should be encouraged unless a commissioner's information request would require significant staff time for them to get the information. In that case, the request should be made to the director.
- Staff should not be allowed to make requests for commission action except through the agency director.
- Commissioners should refrain from providing "advice" to the staff or to the agency director. The staff and the director are capable of determining who to ask for advice and, at their own discretion, can ask commissioners for their opinions. Commissioners offering unsolicited advice make it difficult for the director and staff to distinguish advice from direction.

- Commissions speak with **one voice.** If the commission takes a majority vote, then the decision is clear direction to the agency director. Should a minority of commissioners disagree, they aren't permitted to approach the agency director to get actions in their favor. This prevents different and conflicting directions given by individual commissioners.

Speaking with one voice does not mean unanimity among commission members. In fact, commission members are likely to disagree over important issues. The best practice when making decisions by commission vote is that referred to as "disagree and commit." This means that if a commissioner was among the minority in the vote on a decision, that individual commissioner has three responsibilities:

1. When asked by others about the commission's vote, to explain the rationale of the commission.
2. Align his or her individual resources with the decision (100 percent compliance with no sabotaging or negative comments about the decision).
3. Seek contrary evidence to the decision without sabotaging and bring this evidence back to the group if the first decision does not work.

The only possible exception to this approach is if a commissioner believes a law is being broken.

Commission Role 6: Commission Governance— *How the Commission Governs Itself*

Until now, the commission roles, fulfilled by developing policies, have dealt with the commission's relationship to the agency. The commission also needs to make policies governing how it works together as a whole, and as individual commissioners.

Policies governing commission processes can vary, but they often include such directives as the following examples:

Commissioners will:

1. Come prepared to meetings, having read all materials sent to them, etc.;
2. Be respectful of other commissioners, the director, and the director's staff in all interactions and especially in public meetings. This does

not mean that there can't be strong disagreements but that these differences are voiced professionally;

3. Consider the overall statewide benefit when making decisions and place this benefit above specific geographic or interest group representation;

4. Be explicit about the values used in making decisions;

5. Recuse themselves from decisions where there is a potential for personal conflict of interest;

6. Support commission decisions even when losing the vote on a decision. In other words, no public displays of sour grapes.

For example, here are two real cases that illustrate the potential for problems when only one of the above policies is neglected. Both these cases deal with policy number five: commissioner's conflict of interest.

CASE EXAMPLE: TURKEY DECOYS

A particular state had game regulations in place that forbade the use of decoys for turkey hunting. This regulation had been in place for some time and was generally supported by the agency and its constituents. A new commissioner was appointed who owned a business that manufactured turkey decoys. This commissioner lobbied tirelessly to change the anti-decoy regulation. It was an obvious conflict of interest and detracted from the stature and trust the whole commission had enjoyed with its publics. This one commissioner eventually got his way, to the disgust of many.

CASE EXAMPLE: ELK HUNTING AND OUTFITTING

A second example of conflict of interest occurred in a western state with regulations in place for a concurrent bull and cow elk-hunting season. A new commissioner, who owned a ranch that outfitted for bull elk hunters, did not want to have the cow and bull seasons concurrent. His rationale was that he did not want his high-paying bull elk hunters potentially disrupted by much lower paying cow elk hunters. This new commissioner lobbied heavily and, eventually successfully, to institute a late-season cow-only hunt in the area of the state where his ranch was located. This was not well received by many agency staff, and many public hunters viewed it as unfairly allocating benefits to the outfitting business and as promoting privatization of wildlife in the state. This one commissioner's action was seen as self-serving and it eroded the public's trust with the entire nine-member commission.

Commissions' reluctance to address errant behaviors of individual commissioners is a particularly thorny issue. This is a parallel to the supervisor's classic dilemma of needing to correct an errant employee. There is a natural tendency to want to avoid conflict. The fact that commissions have to confront a member of their exclusive group, and the power of individual members of a commission, make the discipline of addressing individual's errant behaviors even harder.

My experience has been that commissions can be pretty good about agreeing on what governance processes will be used, sometimes even writing them in the form of policies. Most of the commissions I have dealt with seem to have a "good old boys club" modus operandi of not disagreeing publicly if it can be helped, and certainly not disciplining a board member for acting outside policy. This leads to a breakdown of the power of the policy process and commission discipline in general. John Carver's experience mirrors mine. He states, "It is as if the statement of intention is sufficient to fulfill the discipline. This does not work for dieting or mowing the lawn—and it won't work for governance" (Carver 1997).

Mike Fraidenburg (pers. comm.) describes one of the least confrontational ways for commissioners to address individual behaviors. He recommends commissions jointly develop a personal performance questionnaire. Then, once a year, the commissioners anonymously evaluate each other so each commissioner receives peer feedback on performance. This way, if bad behavior is a problem, at least the offending commissioners know how they are affecting their colleagues. I encourage commissions to use the practice of drafting a statement in which all commissioners agree to help hold each other accountable when trying to adhere to commission behavior and protocol policies. Helping to hold each other accountable requires courage, and often tact, but provides an agreed-upon way to broach the sensitive subject of misbehaviors.

If individual commissioner behavior requires a stronger approach, then the rest of the commissioners need to meet with the offending commissioner in an intervention process. They explain the problems that the errant behaviors are causing and what actions the rest of the commissioners will need to take if it continues. Such actions can include, for example, asking the governor to intervene or for removal of the errant commissioner. Each case will be different depending on relationships and the power of the individuals involved. Solutions will need to be tailored to each case. The point is that a commission cannot afford to ignore disciplining of its members when enforcing governance policies. Courage is mandatory.

In this next section I'll discuss some specific issues that commissions commonly have to address.

Handling Mandated Decisions that are Out of Sync with Commission Roles

Commissions fulfill their six roles by using just **four** categories of policies: 1) ends, 2) means, (executive limits on operational means), 3) commission–director/staff linkage and 4) commission self-governance process. If only these four categories of policies are used, then how do commissions handle the more commonly addressed topics like line-item budget approvals or setting regulations for fish and wildlife?

Approving the line-item budget and regulation setting are holdover duties from an era when commissions had no roadmap for governance by using policies. Historically, the "right thing" was to have the commission approve the line-item budget and make individual game regulations. Many states have laws requiring that the commission still approve budgets and land purchases, set game regulations, and occasionally conduct other specific tasks. Using a policy governance approach simplifies these decisions. Let's look at two instances when decisions are statutorily required of the commission and how policy governance can be used.

Budget Approval Decisions

What usually happens with budget approval by commissions is that the agency staff develops a voluminous document with great detail about the budget. This document is then given to the commissioners for approval. Commissioners are part-time and do not have the time to pore over the dozens of pages of details and try to understand the arcane accounting processes. But commissions don't want to rubber stamp the budget either, so they revert to nitpicking. They look for things they can pick out that are understandable and question them in order to avoid rubber-stamping the process. This gives the appearance of fiduciary responsibility, but really it's a very ineffective process for budget oversight and it is certainly an ineffective way for the commission to use the budget as a broad, direction-setting tool.

Using a policy governance approach avoids commissioners reviewing a line-item budget listing and instead allows them to request a proposed **budget report** from the director that gives a summary of each program's costs and expected benefits. For each program, the report includes an explanation of how the proposed budget is to be spent in **compliance with commission policies.** This specifically addresses such policies as how the budget meets commission expectations for effectiveness, for financial risk, and other policies that are applicable.

Rather than reviewing line-item budget allocations, commissioners review this report to determine how much is spent for what ends and decide whether the balance among competing priorities is acceptable. The commission occupies itself with larger questions such as: "Are these programs a good bang for the buck?" and "Do they serve the right constituents in the right amounts?" This process of asking, essentially, "Does this budget comply with our policies?" is much more effective than nitpicking voluminous pages of data.

The Sirens' Song of Setting Regulations

How can a commission meet its legal obligations to set regulations when using policies to govern? Normally, the agency proposes the regulations, commissions hear public comment, and then the commissions pass, amend, or deny regulations. But this level of detail is below the level at which a commission needs to operate.

Admittedly, regulation setting is a seductive process—easy to be drawn into because it is fun, fulfills personal passions of commissioners, and, most of all, provides a sense of accomplishment because it is a concrete action. It is easy (seductive) to step into this quicksand that draws the commission into a greater and greater minutiae of details. This effectively usurps time and focus from the larger questions only the commission can handle. Commissions need to **exhibit the discipline** required to avoid this seductive trap.

So how is this accomplished? Commissioners often unthinkingly accept that the statutory requirements to set regulations means actually voting on seasons, bag limits, and so on. The commissioners fail to realize that in at least some states they can also fulfill their statutory obligations by setting sideboards (policies) governing regulations and thus, controlling regulation setting instead of voting on each regulation individually. To do this, the commission asks the director to submit a **report** about how the proposed new regulations meet the policies of the commission, for example, policies regarding protection of the natural resources and fair distribution of, say, hunting opportunity.

If the commission concludes that the regulations proposed are within commission policies, then the regulations are considered pre-approved. After all, the commission has already made its policies as to ends and means, so as long as the regulations fall within policy they do not need further commission consideration. Remember, the agency director is the one responsible for achieving the desired results (ends) defined by the commission. Consequently, the commission cannot set all the regulations and still expect to hold the agency director accountable for achieving the results for fish and wildlife.

In summary, a commission discussion of regulations should center on these two questions:

1. Are the applicable commission policies met by these regulations?
2. Are the monitoring processes acceptable—can the commission monitor whether regulations are working?

Fear not—the commission can still hear public testimony related to policies such as those regarding equity of opportunity, resource protection, and results achieved. If some regulation is found to be outside policy, then the commission can mandate the director bring back a revised proposal or the commissioners can amend the proposed regulation themselves. The point is that each regulation is not reviewed in a vacuum but is reviewed in the context of how it meets existing policies. The regulation is compared against policies describing results to be achieved, means utilized, and ability of results to be monitored.

The difference in the policy governance process and the way most commissions deal with regulations is that, currently, commissions make numerous individual regulatory decisions without any clear overall policy. This leads to haphazard decision-making spurred by individual commissioner concerns or special-interest-group lobbying. The result is an accumulation of numerous complex regulations over time that is difficult for even professional agency staff to understand.

As an example, I was conducting a training workshop for a Rocky Mountain state fish and wildlife agency. A conservation officer read their pheasant hunting regulations to a group of twenty-five agency staff. The regulations included special exceptions for youth hunters, special area exceptions, and numerous other nuances that resulted in not one of the agency's professional staff being able to understand what was and was not legal for pheasant hunting in their state. Many other examples of convoluted and even contradictory regulations abound as a result of commission regulation setting on a case-by-case basis without any overall policy direction.

A better alternative is to set overall policies and then monitor regulation changes to determine whether or not they achieve the intention of the policies in place. This process provides a clear basis for regulation decisions and also provides guidance to the agency director and his or her staff for proposing future regulations, while keeping the commission out of day-to-day management minutiae. Very importantly, the public attending regulation-setting meetings and the agency director and staff will more clearly understand why specific regulations were accepted, amended or rejected.

The Fallacy of Commissions Approving Agency Plans and Programs

While it is fine for a commission to approve an overall agency strategic plan, sometimes the director or staff brings specific program plans to the commission for approval. An example may be a statewide deer management plan, or a major stream fisheries plan. The director is responsible for ensuring that programs within the agency are within commission policy. While commission approval may seem "nice to do," it has subtle but very damaging effects. Once commission approval is received for a program, then later, if program changes are needed, the staff must wait until the commission finds time to meet again and approve the changes. This makes adjustments to plans cumbersome and slow.

More importantly, if the commission approves the program plans, it amounts to the commission **prescribing** what should be done. If the program fails and the commission has approved the plan, then the commission cannot hold anyone but itself accountable. The director and his staff should be responsible for deciding how best to accomplish program ends as long as the means do not include unacceptable methods as defined by commission policy. By not approving plans, the commission retains its role of deciding desired results (ends) and stating unacceptable means, while the director and agency staff retain their roles of deciding how to best accomplish the results and the responsibility for program success or failure. Commissions evaluate the effectiveness of their agency programs not by approving the program plans, but instead by requiring **monitoring reports** on programs' progress and success or failure.

Commission Chair Versus Agency Director Responsibilities

Commission chair and agency director responsibilities are separate! The director's responsibility is to manage day-to-day agency operations to achieve the results designated by the commission while ensuring that unacceptable means are avoided. The commission chair's responsibility is to see that the commission adheres to its own governance process policies and adheres to policies of delegation and interaction set forth in commission–director/staff linkage policies. What this means is that commission management is the responsibility of the commission chair and the agency management is the responsibility of the director. This separation of responsibility is frequently violated in the ways commissions and directors currently operate. The most common example is in setting the commission's agenda governing what they will address in any particular meeting.

Who Sets the Commission Agenda

Staff must not take on commission work such as designing the commission's agenda. It should be up to the commission to decide which policies to review and refine at the next meeting and which monitoring reports to require. Frequently, agency directors and their staff construct the commission agenda or at least have major input into what items are on the agenda. It is little wonder that many commission agendas are then filled with staff items such as program approvals, document approvals, and budget items. Mostly this is not intentionally nefarious or deceitful behavior. But this process gives the director and staff undue control over the commission's focus. At worst, directors manipulate their commissioners through the agenda-setting process.

Commissions end up being stage managed by the director and his staff when, instead, it should be the commission's role to set its own agenda and address the larger, more important issues of what should be the desired results, at what cost, and for whom. Monitoring agency progress on results is another important role for commissions that is seldom addressed when the director and agency staff set the commission agendas. How many times in the last year has your commission requested a monitoring report on an agency program?

The agency has specific items like hunting seasons, fishing seasons, and annual budget cycles that recur annually, requiring commission consideration and approval within certain times periods each year. I suggest rather than allowing this to be the driver for who sets the commission agenda, that the commission request recurring annual deadlines from the agency so the commission can consider them when designing its own meeting agendas throughout the year.

Many commissions and their chairs prefer to be relieved of the responsibilities for developing agendas and for dealing with the hard questions related to the agency ends and means. Certainly it is much easier to deal with issues as they arise and make spur-of-the-moment decisions without having to adhere to overall policies and values that have been clearly defined. Without clear policies, the potential still remains to use commission power and authority, it just happens without much structure or role specification.

This approach is one of the major problems with commissions today, resulting in a process in which commissions regularly fail to achieve their full potential and value to an agency. For example, two state fish and wildlife commissions with which I worked (one in the Northeast and another in the West) explored the opportunity to use a policy governance process instead of staying buried in day-to-day minutiae. Each commission had a few individual members who were truly excited about the prospects of doing a broader, more critical job. But in both cases the remaining commission members were lukewarm to the changes required and much more comfortable with using familiar past processes. In the end, neither commission changed its old behaviors and both avoided confronting the broader, more important issues only commissions can address.

Developing Commission Policies

Ask yourself these questions: "Does my commission have a set of written policies? Does anyone know where these written policies are? When was the last time they were used in making decisions?" Many commissions have some written policies. These policies are usually a hodgepodge buried in various commission minutes and not readily accessible. Commission policies should be clearly documented and in a central location for reference. Each commissioner needs to have a copy readily available. When using a system of commission governance by policies, **all** commission decisions are guided by referring to policies written by the commission.

There are many things to learn if a commission wants to improve its policies and embark on the process of policy governance. It is beyond the scope of this chapter to cover them all, but two important considerations are the policy size and specificity.

A. Policies of Different Sizes

One concern of commissions is that they will omit something important when writing policies. Fortunately, policies come in different sizes. The solution to the concern of omission is to write the largest, overarching policies first in each of the four categories 1) results (ends), 2) executive limits on operational means, 3) commission–director/staff linkage, and 4) commission self-governance processes. These large, overarching policies are intended to cover everything so that nothing is left out, and then more specific concerns can be addressed. Examples are shown below.

EXAMPLES OF THREE LEVELS OF RESULTS POLICIES:
Level 1 (Broadest): The agency does what it is supposed to for the citizens of the state.

Level 2: The agency provides recreational opportunities for all citizens, with an equal chance for participation.

Level 3: All license-holding hunters within the state have an equal opportunity to draw for limited permits.

EXAMPLES OF THREE LEVELS OF
EXECUTIVE LIMITATIONS POLICIES
Level 1 (Broadest): The executive director shall not allow any behaviors that are illegal, immoral, or irresponsible.

Level 2: The director shall not spend more than the agency takes in during any fiscal year.

Level 3: The director shall not spend more than fair market costs for materials and equipment.

B. Policy Specificity

After the commission writes the largest level policies for each of the four categories of policies, then the commission can begin to become more specific. How specific should the commission become? Only as specific as needed to ensure that any reasonable interpretation of the policy will be sufficient. In some areas, commissioners may be satisfied with broad level policies, while in other areas they may wish to make more detailed policies.

The commission is encouraged to spell out its expectations only to a level so that *any reasonable interpretation of the policy* will be satisfactory. To go further into details is not required and only increases costs and time required to carry out the policy. For example, if I were to ask a bagel shop waiter for a bagel and I didn't care what kind, then I would just ask for a bagel. The waiter's task is simple—bring me a bagel, any bagel. But if I ask for an organic, whole wheat, blueberry bagel with cream cheese and honey, then the waiter may take much longer to get the correct bagel, and the price may be much higher. Commissions create delays and add cost by being more specific than necessary in policy development.

Basic Policies that Benefit Any Commission

Whether or not a commission decides to completely plunge into governance by policy, there are some basic policies from which any commission can benefit. I have previously mentioned that one of the most common requests I receive from commissions is how to deal with one or a few commissioners who don't adhere to proper protocols. One specific instance involved a commissioner in the Southeast who regularly complained in the media about commission decisions with which he did not agree. This was a major issue that created strife in the commission and made solidarity impossible on controversial issues. The result was that commission decisions were weakened and public perception was that the commission could not get its act together or agree on anything. Public support dwindled markedly for that commission.

This example illustrates why the category of commission *self-governance policies* is very important: *Is it okay for those commissioners who lost a vote on a commission action to go to the press with their complaints? What disciplinary actions will be available?* What are the protocols for commissioner treatment of staff in public meetings, etc.? If a commission has not developed written policies to address these kinds of questions, then it leaves itself open to unrestrained, individual commissioner actions.

The second category of policies from which any commission can benefit is that of commission–director/staff linkage. Previously I have mentioned there are numerous instances where commissioners individually instructed the director or staff to take actions that other commissioners disagreed with or were unaware of. This puts the director and staff in an untenable position. They are faced with following directives from one or a few commissioners and hoping the rest of the commission will not disapprove or find out.

The only other alternative for the director and staff is to tattle and upset the lone wolf commissioner. It's a losing situation for the director and staff. However, everyone benefits when procedures are made clear on how the agency director and staff are to receive direction from the commission, that is, by majority vote and not by individual commissioner. All benefit when the roles for staff and commissioners are clearly specified, preventing staff from getting involved in doing commission work and commissioners from attempting to "help" staff.

The good news is that simply addressing some basic policies in these two categories can alleviate many of the common problems I see in my work with agencies and their commissions. Of course, any commission must have the discipline to follow its own policies for them to be effective. Remember, intent alone does not work for mowing the yard, losing weight, or effectively functioning as a commission. Having basic, written policies and the discipline to follow them will prevent a host of problems like the bullying described at the beginning of this chapter.

Summary

Problems between commissions and agencies are often the result of poorly thought-out processes for commission governance. This creates confusion over power and an atmosphere of mutual distrust. The best way to overcome these problems is to use a system of policies that clarifies purpose for the agency and for the commission, the roles of each, and the levels of authority for each.

The agency director has five major roles:

1. Achievement of desired results (ends) produced by the agency
2. Control of day-to-day operations of the agency
3. Supervision of agency employees
4. Ensuring that all means used by the agency and its employees are acceptable to the commission
5. Fiscal responsibility by conforming to a balanced budget

The commission has six roles:

1. Linkage of the agency with the fish and wildlife "owners" (citizens of the state)
2. Defining the agency's desired results (ends) to be achieved for which constituencies
3. Specifying means that are unacceptable to achieve the ends
4. Delegation of responsibility for achieving specified results and ensuring director-agency performance
5. Specifying the commission–director/staff linkage
6. Specifying how the commission governs itself

Commissions need to develop policies that define these roles and separate powers between the commission and the agency director and staff.

Commissions actually increase their overall reach and control of agency strategic direction when they use a system of governance that develops policies focused on their six roles listed above. Monitoring reports are the means by which the commission can oversee work in an agency at the appropriate level and refrain from micromanaging the agency.

While good commission policy governance is critical to maximizing agency effectiveness, there are often times when changes within the agency are needed. Making major changes within an agency is a daunting task for an agency director, and there is no guarantee of success. The next chapter addresses stages of change and gives some guidance to directors for maximizing the success of change efforts.

Literature Cited

Carver, John. 1997. *Boards that Make a Difference*. Jossey-Bass. San Francisco, CA. 241 pp.

Carver, John and Miriam Carver. 1997. *Reinventing Your Board*. Jossey-Bass. San Francisco, CA. 232 pp. See also: www.carvergovernance.com/index.html.

Case, David J. and Phil T. Seng. 1999. *Agency Reputation and Credibility*. David J. Case and Assoc. Mishawaka, IN. 24 pp.

Jacobsen, Cynthia A. 2008. "Wildlife Conservation and Management in the 21st Century: Understanding Challenges for Institutional Transformation." Ph.D. Diss. Cornell Univ. Syracuse, NY. 147 pp.

Duda, Mark Damian; Steven J. Bissell; and Kira C. Young. 1998. *Wildlife and the American Mind: Public Opinion and Attitudes Toward Fish and Wildlife Management*. Responsive Management. Harrisonburg, VA. 804 pp.

Sax, Joseph L. 1970. "The Public Trust Doctrine in Natural Resource Law: Effective Judicial Intervention." *Michigan Law Review*. The Michigan Law Review Association. 68 (3), pp. 471–566.

CHAPTER FOUR

Changing the Agency

T he point of making changes in an agency is to improve things, perhaps to move from good to excellent or to fix a problem. The demands for change vary from politically driven motives, where an incoming administration believes that the previous political party had things all screwed up, to self-selected changes where an agency sees room for self-improvement. An example of the former often takes the shape of changes in key agency personnel. These new personnel often have "marching orders" to make specific changes to correct problems perceived by the new administration. Examples of the latter may be the desire to broaden agency constituencies to be more inclusive of a larger part of the state's citizens that do not hunt of fish. This may be a desire to increase relevancy to all publics and engender greater public support.

Other self-induced change examples include seeking greater control, greater efficiency, or greater effectiveness in agency operations. The desire for improvements can be fueled by dissatisfaction with just being "good" as an agency. Jim Collins summed up this concept with his statement, "Good is the enemy of great" (Collins 2001).

Regardless of whether agency change is driven by internal or external motivations, the implementers of successful change have a difficult task ahead of them. This became all too clear to me twenty-five years ago when I accepted a job requiring me to implement major change in a state fish and wildlife agency.

It was the second week of my new job and early in the morning. I had just gotten out of bed. I looked in the mirror and shook my head. "What have I gotten myself into?" I asked myself. I had given up a great wildlife job with a major university in another state to take this new one with a state fish and wildlife agency. But now, after only a few days, I realized what a momentous task was ahead of me. I felt woefully unprepared. I was now the new guy in the agency, and I came from out-of-state. I wasn't "one of them" and, my arrival was preceded by a long history of previous failed attempts to bring about change within this agency. Open resistance as well as clandestine and passive resistance were rampant.

At this precarious moment, a quote kept coming to mind from the early 1500s by Niccolo Machiavelli in his book, *The Prince*:

> It must be realized that there is nothing more difficult to plan, more uncertain of success, or more dangerous to manage than the establishment of a new order of government; for he who introduces it makes enemies of all those who derived advantage from the old order and finds lukewarm defenders among those who stand to gain from the new one (Machiavelli 2003).

On the plus side, I had the blessing of the agency director to do what was needed to bring about the desired changes. The director wanted me to implement a new system of management that would give him greater ability to direct the agency, greater management oversight, and better budgeting accountability. My challenge in this instance was to implement a totally new method of operating the agency based upon instituting work plans for all agency expenditures. This change would affect how the agency built its budget and accounted for the expenditure of funds on each project. It also increased the accountability of all project managers.

I had no authority over anyone other than a part-time secretary who assisted me. Naively, I had anticipated the whole project would take only two to three years. I was so wrong! After **seven** years of working very hard, the new method for operating the agency was finally institutionalized. This occurred even after my fumbling and mistakes while learning to bring about the change. While this experience was difficult, it was a great first-hand learning experience! I gained great understanding of how formidable a challenge major change can be for an agency.

In this chapter I will share with you some of the things I learned with that state fish and wildlife agency and during my fifteen years working with the Association of Fish and Wildlife Agencies Management Assistance Team helping other state fish and wildlife agencies across the nation implement change. I can't offer a panacea, just some proven, practical insights. The focus in this chapter is on making *major* change, not just incremental changes. As Goss, et al. (1993) observed, "Incremental change isn't enough for many companies today. They don't need to change what is; they need to create what isn't." This is the magnitude and type of change I will address.

Let's begin by first, taking a hard look at determining **when** a major agency change is actually needed and how to make the strategic decisions necessary. Dr. Margaret Wheatley (pers. comm.) first introduced me to a very helpful tool for this. She called it the U Curve. Andy Grove (1999) in his book *Only the Paranoid Survive*, refers to this same concept as "the inflection point." It describes when an organization first begins to decline in the products and services offered to constituents or the organization's financial health, effectiveness, etc. This is the point where change is required.

In the following U Curve diagram, the horizontal axis represents time and the vertical axis represents any potential factors of concern, such as declining service to constituents, declining agency size, declining financial health, and/or declining public or political support. The solid line illustrates steady growth in one or more of the agency effectiveness factors over time until it reaches the point where growth begins to level off, followed by decline. This is the inflection point (thick black arrow). Most government agencies cannot respond quickly once they have arrived at this point.

There is almost always a period of time before the declining trend can be recognized as real, not just a minor fluctuation. This is why the decision point marked by the slender arrow in the graph does not occur right at the inflection point but some time after it.

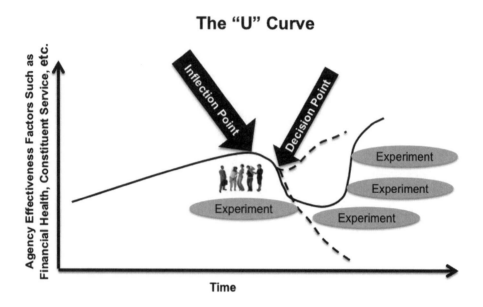

The "U" Curve

Determining When Major Change is Needed

At the decision point, an assessment is needed that answers the question: "What do we think will happen in the future?" If the expectation is that the situation will get better and right itself, then the strategy typically is for an agency to keep doing what it's been doing and perhaps do it more feverishly. The dashed line that curves upward and ultimately resumes the normal slope of growth in effectiveness for the agency represents this expectation.

However, the other option is that the current decline is not likely to right itself and things will not get better without some change by the agency. This is represented in the graph by the dashed line that continues downward from the decision point. If this is the expectation, then the agency must make major changes if it expects to survive.

There are three important points here. First, there are no certain answers! The strategic decision made at the decision point is based on your best guess. No one knows what will happen in the future. Second, inflection points arrive subtly; they arrive on "little cat's feet" (Grove 1999). There is no blaring band or single crisis that announces the slow, insidious decline of the agency. For example, many fish and wildlife agencies

Inflection Point

have watched a slow decline in license sales over the last decade or so. Based upon this and an increasingly urban public's changing attitudes away from hunting and fishing toward non-consumptive wildlife interests like wildlife watching, Cynthia Jacobsen (2008) pointed out the need for agency change among many state fish and wildlife agencies.

In my opinion, many of these agencies have arrived at, or are now past, the optimum point for making a strategic decision whether or not to change. While I don't believe it is too late, I suggest that state fish and wildlife agencies strongly consider without delay addressing their situation in this regard. Consider what part of your state's citizen population your agency is serving, what tough choices can be made to increase your agency's relevancy to **all** publics, and at what risks will you undertake these potential changes.

Third, ignoring significant changes, like declines in the agency's license sales, is a decision in itself. It represents choosing the path of only hoping that things will get better while keeping the agency just doing what it's done in the past. The strategic decision point is too dangerous a place in the growth cycle of an agency to make the decision by default. A conscious decision based on the best information available is needed.

Consider the past history of agency ups and downs—is the current status just a normal fluctuation? What about the current culture and values of the agency—is it stagnant and no longer as relevant to today's environs for the agency? What has changed in the agency's surrounding influences—for example have there been major changes in citizens' preferences, desires, and expectations of the agency over time and has the agency responded to these changes successfully?

Six Reasons for Failure to Make Strategic Agency Change Decisions

Multiple factors are at play that causes many top-level decision-makers to avoid making the strategic decisions for agency change when needed.

1. **Optimization for Efficiency:** Any agency that has been around for long is optimized for efficiency rather than for agility. The agency has become focused on efficiently doing what has made it effective in the first place. Agility is the ability to capitalize on opportunities and to dodge threats with speed and assurance (Kotter 2012). This means that the agency must change its focus from **efficiency** to overall **agility and effectiveness** with constituents in order to be able to successfully consider strategic changes.

2. **Shaky Long-Term Survival:** Governors often appoint state agency directors. This means that a four-year term is the horizon of concern for most governors and agency directors. Two terms of eight years are only a possibility and not guaranteed. Keeping order in the political system and not creating dissent among stakeholders is the strategy for reelection and for reappointment of directors. Making a major change in an agency certainly will engender dissidence and strife. Frequently, avoiding dissidence for the immediacy of political survival and reelection or reappointment are chief factors dwarfing the more important long-term strategic concerns of the agency.

   In some states, a commission selects the agency director, but the governor appoints the commission members. Even though commissioners are usually appointed in staggered terms and/or with bipartisan requirements for commission makeup, the same concerns and influences are present for commissions, albeit perhaps to a lesser degree. Ron Regan, executive director of the Association of Fish and Wildlife Agencies, estimates that the average tenure of a state fish and wildlife agency director is only two and a half years due to gubernatorial changes and other related issues (pers. comm.). It's hard to take the long view when long-term survival is so shaky.

3. **The Trap of Past Success:** Success is really its own trap! Successful agencies got there by doing what made them successful. Changing—doing something new and different—seems illogical to most people in a successful agency, even when circumstances all around the agency have changed. Business strategist Roger Martin sums it up well when he says, "Companies don't make the most of new opportunities because they're making the most of old ones" (Martin 1993).

4. **Success Can't be Guaranteed:** There is no guarantee of success when choosing to make a major agency change. As Goss, et al. (1993) states, "The journey to reinvent yourself and your company is a sink-or-swim proposition." Greiner, et al. (2002) adds, "Numerous studies show that most authority figures fail in their attempts to change organizations."

5. **Uncertainty Too High:** The uncertainty of whether the agency is at an inflection point weakens the courage of many to take the bold steps necessary for change. As mentioned before, inflection points come on little cat's feet. There is no loud storm warning, no news flash. It comes as slow, subtle changes in the agency's constituents and operating environment that must be perceived without concrete proof that the changes are not temporary but major and permanent.

6. **Leadership Required:** Change requires leadership. John Kotter (1996) says, "Successful transformation is 70 to 90 percent leadership and only 10 to 30 percent management." As noted in Chapter Five of this book, Leadership is a dangerous undertaking. Many in high positions lack the courage to take on a major change initiative because they have spent their careers rising to the level they now enjoy and they have too much to lose if they create dissidence in the agency and the political system. At a minimum, leadership has been historically lacking because agency authority figures did not have the training to exhibit good leadership. Although that is changing, true leadership still remains elusive.

With all these factors at play it's understandable that high-ranking agency officials may be reluctant to choose the path of implementing major agency change. However, "feeling safe and being safe are two different things" (Lawler, et al. 2006). The long-term effects of a failure to change can mean agency decline and eventual irrelevance. After all, your fish and wildlife agency does not have a right to exist! It exists only because it serves the needs of one or more publics. If the needs and expectations of those publics change over time, the agency cannot ignore them and expect continued success. For example, if constituents change their expectations and desires to include more wildlife watching, use of management areas for picnicking, horseback riding, and other non-consumptive activities, then what are the **long-term** ramifications if your agency refuses to adjust to meet these expectations, even though groups of hunters and anglers may resist any change?

Waiting too long to change presents its own hazards. If the agency waits too long, then it may not have the support or the resources necessary to bring about a successful change. Grove (1996) reports from his experience with changing the Intel Company that waiting caused more angst and implementation required harsher actions than if those actions had been taken earlier. My experience with agencies waiting too long to initiate change is similar to Grove's findings. The former director of the Florida Fish and Wildlife Conservation Commission, Ken Haddad, (pers. comm.) told me, "In today's world change should/could be synonymous with continual improvement and be a cultural norm for agency staff based on arguably a rapidly changing constituency in the wildlife world. Agencies are slow to change and often fail to recognize that they must bring the constituents together (traditional with non-traditional)."

Once the decision is made to implement a major agency change, it's like starting a long trek across an unchartered arctic landscape. You have a mission, a strategy, and a vision, but there's no detailed roadmap to follow. It's likely that not all of those who begin the journey with you will survive. You have to be prepared and willing to lose some employees over the long trek.

Tough decisions will need to be made while certainty remains an elusive mirage. McEwen and Miniter (2014) provided an example when they described a major organizational shift in the Navy SEALS. The shift was from the early SEALS' rogue culture to a new professional culture. SEALS initially considered themselves superior warriors but somewhat rogues within the Navy system. They exhibited their rogue nature in disregarding many Navy regulations and even in dressing much more casually and wearing long hair. The new SEALS were expected to be professional soldiers with strict regulation adherence similar to the rest of the Navy. This shift was termed *shifting* SEALS *from pirates to professionals*. McEwen and Miniter described this major shift as follows:

> The commander made it clear to the men of the SEAL teams that they had to change or they had to leave. Many did. The old guard

that had served enough time to earn a pension quickly retired. Others stuck it out until they made their twenty years, qualified for a pension, and then they, too, left. Some even departed before they could secure a pension. . . . The cultural shift was too much of a shock. Within four years, most of the old guard—officers and enlisted—were gone. . . . A new SEAL team culture emerged.

The U Curve graph indicates the decision to institute change with the solid black line extending downward past the decision point. This represents the fact that just the decision to change does not create the change nor stop the downward decline of the agency.

It takes experimentation with new methods of operation and creation of new products and services to meet changing customer needs and expectations. It's also important to note that the first experiments should be just that—experiments! Some failures are normal and continued downward decline is likely. It may be advantageous at this point to remember a quote by Franklin D. Roosevelt during the Great Depression when he was looking at experimentation to find answers. He said, "It is common sense to take a method and try it: If it fails, admit it frankly and try another. But above all, try something" (Roosevelt 1932).

While Roosevelt makes a common-sense case for experimentation, his words should not be taken to mean pulling things out of thin air or random experiments encompassing anything that is different from what your agency normally does. Experimentation needs to be guided by your knowledge of the nature of the external changes that are affecting your agency.

These changes can be varied, with examples ranging from changing demographics, where wildlife recreationists are aging and less physically able, to populations of citizens becoming more urbanized or suburbanized and demands or expectations for managing nuisance wildlife increase while hunting and angling demands decrease. Your understanding of these types of changes should guide your continued experimentation with changes in agency products and services until enough is learned to experience some successes. Then, add fuel to the fires that burn the brightest. It's only at this point that the agency can expect to stop the downward trend, level off, and begin the climb back up the U Curve to a trajectory of improved constituent service, financial health, etc.

The stages of experimentation, creating change from a certain past to the uncertain future, and getting the employees to actually implement the changes are much easier if your agency employees have high trust levels among themselves and with management. This creates a cohesive work environment (Covey 2006). This concept is represented on the U Curve by the images of people grouped together at the inflection and decision points.

Successfully Implementing Changes Mandated from Outside the Agency

Not all change initiatives are produced from within an agency. Sometimes you have to make successful changes mandated by other government or political entities. My work helping the Florida Fish and Wildlife Conservation Commission (FWC) implement a major agency change was another rich learning opportunity for me on the challenges of change. The FWC change effort dealt with implementing a merger politically mandated by constitutional amendment between the former offices of the Marine Fisheries Commission, Division of Marine Resources, and the Division of Law Enforcement of the Florida Department of Environmental Protection, and all of the employees and commissioners of the former Game and Freshwater Fish Commission. This was an enormous task led by Ken Haddad, who became executive director of the FWC two years after the merger was mandated and at which point FWC had no strategic plan and was composed of parts and pieces of agencies with no coherent direction. After an extensive constituent-based planning process, it became clear that more major change was needed to complete the merger and implement new direction.

I helped Director Haddad and his top-level administrators outline steps for bringing about completion of this merger. It required great leadership from Ken and his staff. Fortunately, they were up to the task and provided the leadership necessary for success.

During this time I introduced Ken and his staff to some of the works of John Kotter, a professor at Harvard's School of Business. Specifically, I encouraged the Florida staff to use Kotter's eight stages for leading change that the author describes in his book *Leading Change* (Kotter 1996).

The Eight-Stage Change Process

The eight stages in the change process (Kotter 1996) are listed below in sequential order:

1. Establishing a sense of urgency.
2. Creating the guiding coalition.
3. Developing a vision and strategy.
4. Communicating the change vision.
5. Empowering broad-based action.
6. Generating short-term wins.
7. Consolidating gains and producing more change.
8. Anchoring new approaches in the culture.

No endeavor is as simple as these eight stages might seem. However, these eight stages do provide a **framework** for focusing effort as you implement major changes. Also, the sequence of the stages outlined is very important. For example, establishing a sense of urgency should be addressed **first.** Otherwise, complacency will likely overcome all other efforts. With that said, the process of using the eight stages is not just a rote, by-the-numbers process. Instead, it is a process that will unfold at different stages in different parts of the agency, and sometimes they will occur simultaneously. Jeanie Duck, noted change expert and author, perhaps said it best when she stated, "Managing change is like balancing a mobile. Achieving this critical balance means managing the conversation between the people leading the change effort and those who are expected to implement the new strategies; creating an organizational context in which change can occur; and managing emotional connections, which have traditionally been banned from the workplace but are essential for a successful transformation" (Duck 1993). She refers to emotional connections by stating, "Change is fundamentally about feelings; companies that want their workers to contribute with their heads and hearts have to accept that emotions are essential to the new management" (Duck 1993).

Stage 1. Establish a Sense of Urgency

The sense of urgency was well established early on in the FWC. The merger had already been mandated. It was not a choice for the agencies involved; it was only a matter of how the merger would be implemented. This is not always the case with big changes in agencies. Many times the change is something desired only by the top-level administration of an agency. Implementation is not at all a sure thing. Government agencies are fraught with what Duck calls *change survivors*—people who have learned to survive change programs without actually changing themselves.

The first stage is building a fire under the people who will need to implement the change. Kotter warns not to underestimate the power of complacency. It is enormous. Regarding organizations' failures to bring about change he says, "the number-one problem they have is all about creating a sense of urgency (Kotter 2008)." Creating urgency can be difficult because agencies do not normally exist in a constant state of urgency. This is something that must be created in the organization unless external factors have already conspired to provide this, as was the case with the FWC merger.

It's not enough to patiently wait for a crisis. It may never come. You have to really do your homework to identify a suitable problem to drive the sense of urgency. A suitable problem would be visible, unambiguous, related to real agency issues, and significant enough that small changes or actions will not solve it. Plus, **you** have to **act** with urgency. People watch what you do much more than what you say. For example, what's the message being sent if your meetings to discuss change are interrupted by *more important* matters and you postpone working on the change due to other duties?

Your creation of a sense of urgency is not about creating a false crisis. The urgency must be real, and the task is certainly more than carelessly dumping external realities into an organization in hopes of stimulating some type of action. It's about exercising judgment and reading the ability of the organization to withstand new and disturbing information. Then it's about bringing in this information in its various forms at the time and rate the organization can withstand. For example, FWC held a meeting of its stakeholders—more than 100 organizations—where it became clear that stakeholder interests and needs were not being met by FWC and that the FWC structure was dysfunctional in allowing the agency to meet those constituent needs. FWC staff were presented with this information and informed that radical change was necessary to accommodate the constituents.

It is common to underestimate the stalling power of the "we bes"—those who say, "We be here when you got here and we be here after you're gone." This is particularly common in government agencies where the perception proliferates that you can hire employees into the agency but you can't get them out.

The trap of success is also a major factor contributing to complacency, and the fish and wildlife profession is not immune to falling into this trap. The profession has experienced huge success in bringing wildlife populations back from the abysmal low numbers at the beginning of the twentieth century. These big successes over many years led to wildlife agency staff turning their eyes inward and focusing on greater effectiveness. They focused on what was occurring within the agencies and mostly ignored what was happening outside. This inward focus breeds complacency to any changes that occur outside the agency.

Lastly, creating urgency is often neglected because many top administrators overestimate their power to make change happen. Change occurs when people change their **actions,** their **perceptions,** and how **they feel** about the new activities they perform. This cannot be mandated! Autocratic power can force incremental change in actions, but as you've probably observed, the actions are likely superficial and apt to revert back to the former practices as soon as the authority figure turns his or her head.

Stage 2. Creating a Guiding Coalition

Kotter's second stage in his eight-stage process is that of creating a guiding coalition. The guiding coalition must understand that its job is not to just work on the change initiative as a group but also to work **with** the people they supervise to instill a vision and provide employee engagement so the employees will at least accept, if not desire, the required changes. This often means disappointing your own people at some level—a leadership task that many in authority understandably loathe undertaking.

In addition, the right people must be selected for the guiding coalition. They must have both positional power within the agency and the trust of employees. If the guiding coalition members do not have sufficient positional power, then the change effort is doomed. Many fish and wildlife agencies I have worked with put together guiding coalitions to oversee a significant change, but often these coalitions were composed of mostly mid- and lower-level employees. They did not have the authority, individually or collectively, to make anything stick. Such groups were almost always relegated to seeking approval from above, presenting proposals to make only incremental changes, and gritting their teeth when higher level personnel resisted—a classic case of guiding coalitions with the wrong people on them.

Fortunately, when I worked on implementing major management process changes for the state agency mentioned at the beginning of this chapter, their guiding coalition had sufficient power because it included all the top-level administrators from the agency's headquarters. It provided enough power to lead the change. This power was due not only to coalition members having enough positional power within the agency. They also had the trust and respect of the employees. If employee trust of coalition members is not present, then the coalition will fail even if its members have positional power.

An example of a coalition lacking both positional power and trust occurred when I worked with a state fish and wildlife agency to establish a cooperative effort between the agency and its land grant university. This cooperative program was to be built upon the concept of the agency partnering with organization development experts at the university. The result was to be effective organization management expertise made available to the fish and wildlife agency at below-market costs. I personally knew the organization development experts at the university as well as the agency director and many of his staff. I felt this could be a mutually beneficial arrangement and provide a model for other states and universities to follow. At that time, a number of fish and wildlife agencies had already partnered with universities to gain access to human dimensions expertise, so the concept had been proven successful in at least one field of study.

After a couple of meetings involving myself, the university experts, and the agency upper level management, the groundwork for this inventive new change seemed to be established. Then the director appointed a committee (guiding coalition) to handle implementing this new change. It wasn't long until I began to get feedback from agency staff that they felt the committee was doomed to failure. It seems that the staff member appointed to head up this effort was selected because he had failed at a previous assignment and currently "had nothing to do." This coalition chair lacked the power and the trust of employees. The final result was predictable. The effort at making this important change sputtered and finally died.

Overall, the duties of the guiding coalition are to manage the change in the agency. The coalition members must understand the change needed and why it is needed, and have the leadership skills necessary to pull it off and the courage to exercise the required leadership. This group should also represent a cross-section of the agency as well as the various agency hierarchical levels. As already mentioned, people outside the coalition must be able to trust what they are told about the change. Also, trust among coalition members is very important for the coalition to function successfully as a team. Teamwork is mandatory, and a unified front is critical if the change is to succeed.

Once there is a strong sense of urgency throughout the agency and a strong and credible guiding coalition is established, then Kotter's change process calls for developing a vision (reflecting agency values) and a strategy for the change(s).

Stage 3. Developing a Vision and Strategy

For a public agency, the constituents and their needs and desires for products and services should be the ultimate factor in determining the agency's vision and strategy. Constituent input can be gathered in many ways, including social media, surveys, focus groups, telephone logs, and myriad other methods. This is where human dimension research expertise can be applied very effectively. The responsibility for setting agency direction falls upon the agency director who gathers input from constituents as well as employees.

I recall an example from the years when I was a fish and wildlife agency employee. The director, his deputy, and I were meeting with a consultant to explore how to set a direction for the agency that would guide it over the next five years. The director and his deputy described how they might engage the employees in building a direction from the ground up. Their plan followed the type of democratic approach that was this agency's modus operandi.

The consultant looked the director in the eye and said, "Setting direction is the role of the agency leadership! Don't confuse gathering input from the troops with who is responsible for the direction and the vision" (Virginia Tribe pers. comm.). I was struck by the importance of that statement and have since watched a number of agency administrators try to push down decisions about direction and vision to employees so that everyone helps make the final decision. I believe this is the wrong approach for such decision-making. While it is very important to include employee input, do not confuse seeking input and advice with abdicating decision-making responsibility.

EMPLOYEE INVOLVEMENT

The director and the guiding coalition have broad access to a variety of information and are in a position to see the bigger picture for the future and the change(s) necessary to meet that future. Employees in the trenches have access to detailed information, albeit in a narrower spectrum.

As Gino and Staats (2015) observe, "Frontline employees—the people directly involved in creating, selling, delivering, and servicing offerings, and interacting with customers—are frequently in the best position to spot and solve these types of problems." Also, Gen Xers and Millennia's are noted for desiring input into decisions that affect them. Neglecting even old-school employees leaves room for discontent and lack of buy-in. Just let everyone know that employee input will be valued and welcomed, but the decision will be made at the top! Don't let employees assume that the right to be heard is the same as the right to decide.

Stephen Covey (1989) encourages what he calls "co-missioning," or the process of stepping down the overall agency vision, mission, and values to sub-units of the agency, even to the individual level. Through this process, the overall agency mission, vision, and values are established by the top administration, followed by each sub-unit of the agency developing their own mission, vision, and values within the boundaries of the broader overall agency's mission and values. The process can be continued down through the organizational structure even to the individual level. This is a great way to approach the required embedding, or "owning," of the mission, vision, and values in the agency. The key is that it allows for individual involvement. Individuals can specify what parts of the overall vision and mission they will be responsible for. Remember the axiom, *People support what they help build*!

Also, strategies for implementation of the change should follow the process used for cascading down the mission, vision, and values throughout the agency. It starts at the top as to the overall strategy for the agency, which is developed with many forms of information, including employee input. Then, strategy development can be stepped down similar to the process described above so that each sub-unit and each individual can specify their role (subject to supervisor's approval) in bringing about the change.

At each level in the organization, authority for change implementation may need to be reconsidered in order to flatten the decision-making and render implementing the change more efficient. Remember that you cannot assign responsibility for implementing change at each level in the agency unless you also provide the needed authority at each level.

VISION AS A TOOL

Vision is an important tool for changing agency direction. It provides a verbal picture of what things are like in the agency once the change is complete. It is a means of describing the outcomes and the advantages of the change efforts. I am reminded of Martin Luther King's "I Have a Dream" speech describing people being judged by the strength of their character and not the color of their skin as a vision for civil rights.

Many of those in fish and wildlife see vision as an unscientific concept and just so much blowing smoke. It may be because they've had little vision given them from upper level administration. Or maybe they've experienced only weakly developed or poorly implemented vision. A vision is a powerful tool for painting a word picture of a desirable future. Correct use of this tool can invoke people's values and emotions in support of a change. Learn to use this powerful tool.

VALUES AS A TOOL

Values are an important component of developing a vision of change. The values of the top-level administration and the guiding coalition need to be made clear. As people mature, they seek self-actualization and meaning in their work and their lives (Maslow 1943). Connecting this strong motivational factor of self-actualization is crucial in getting employees to "own" the change vision. The fish and wildlife profession, like many non-governmental organizations, has sets of strong values. Different organizations are committed to saving wildlife, feeding the hungry, and curing cancer, for example.

The real professional world for most of us is the forty to sixty hours per week we spend in our jobs. If employee commitment is to be gained, then that reality must connect to each employee's personal values. Doctor James Kennedy's work at Utah State University showed that fish and wildlife professionals have a "missionary-like zeal" for their work (Kennedy1985). This is a representation of commitment that results from deeply held values related to wildlife. As long as wildlife organizations represent these core values, they can reap the commitment of their employees. The important take away here is that you must tie any change initiative to these values.

Stage 4. Communicating the Change Vision and Strategy

Communication of the change vision, process and what the coalition is doing is absolutely critical and must be done on a **continual basis throughout the change process.** Once input from constituents and employees is analyzed and a vision is decided upon and the agency knows what it is envisioned to look like in the future, what it is to produce, what change is needed, and most importantly why, then that information must be continually communicated to the employees. While the communication may use multiple and varying means, it will need to clearly and succinctly explain four things.

1. What the vision is.
2. What are the values the vision represents.
3. What changes are necessary to fulfill the vision.
4. Why the vision was selected and why the particular changes are needed.

While listening to employee questions and providing clarifying answers are important at this stage in the change process, rolling out this change vision is not a debate between management and the employees. It is a one-way communication. It lets everyone understand how their input has been considered and what is desired and expected for the agency as a whole and why. In other words, there are two stages of communication with employees in a change effort. First, is the two-way communication where employee and constituent input is actively sought. The second stage occurs once all input has been considered and direction decided, and then there is one-way communication giving "marching orders" to employees.

If the above process is used to continually communicate the vision, values, and strategy for the change down through the ranks of the agency, then the stage of communicating the vision for the change can be successful. Kotter (1996) reports, however, that most organizations do not use the process described above thus, often failing to communicate the vision and strategy successfully.

CASE EXAMPLE: COMMUNICATING THE CHANGE

When working on the change process mentioned at the beginning of this chapter I found out the hard way communication is not as easy as one may think. Over the period of a year, I traveled multiple times to all regions of the state in which I worked and visited all the regional offices of the fish and wildlife agency to interact with employees about a change effort. I went to great lengths at regional meetings of employees to explain the change needed. I answered questions and had employees help set timelines. In addition, I worked with the agency director to produce a twenty-minute video that was sent to all the regions to communicate the change needed and each region's roles. I wrote regular updates for the agency's newsletter on progress of the change. I also worked with the administrative staff of all the major divisions of the agency, using regularly scheduled meetings to gather the division administrators' input to develop change strategy and set timeframes. I assumed after a year of this magnitude of effort that the change initiative and the strategy were understood throughout the agency.

The reality was that **awareness** had been established at most levels, but not necessarily **understanding** and certainly not **acceptance.** It all hit the fan when I distributed a computer program to secretarial staff for use in implementing a new method of inputting budgeting information. That's when I found that the efforts I had been consumed with making over the last year had been too little! Most employees were vaguely aware of some change efforts originating at headquarters, but did not see it as affecting them. Those who'd sat back and listened seemed genuinely surprised that change was actually happening! I knew I had a major obstacle to overcome in improving communication.

As a result, it took over two months to get the computer program implemented. I had to enlist the division administrators and a few regional supervisors, who comprised the guiding coalition, to enter the apparent communication vacuum. These division administrators had seen their input to the change process as important, but they'd considered the **communication** of the change process "Dwight's job." After all, wasn't I the agency's official in charge of the change? It was a great learning point for me that you can never communicate enough and also that asking one person to communicate a major change is insufficient!

I do believe that the communication efforts I engaged in would have been more effective if I had been the agency director. Ken Haddad, as director of FWC, used a similar communication process as I had where he traveled to all his agency locations and explained the changes to be implemented in FWC. However, I believe there are additional ways to communicate that greatly enhance the one-person show traveling around the state.

Once I realized how much had **not** been communicated, the agency director and I encouraged each division administrator and regional supervisor to have a meeting with his or her staff and describe the necessity for the change. These meetings described where the agency was in the implementation process. Each administrator and supervisor outlined what was expected of his or her employees and answered questions. Continuation of these efforts by division administrators and regional supervisors on an **individual basis** with employees was also necessary to finally achieve understanding.

The impacts of a single person communicating compared to communication carried out by a group of individuals is further illustrated by the following details: I had met approximately fourteen times with regional employees at regional meetings, written four articles for the agency newsletter, met eighteen times with the guiding coalition of fourteen people, and I wrongly assumed that I had communicated thoroughly.

Consider the follow-up effort when each of the fourteen guiding coalition members met with only two different people on their staff each workday to discuss the change. In two months, that amounts to 1,120 **two-way** communications on a **personal basis.** This is huge compared to my four-teen regional meetings, eighteen coalition meetings, and four articles over a year! In addition, the communications on a personal level were far more effective than the group meetings and newsletter efforts made by only one person. The point is not to underestimate the need to commu-nicate the vision and strategy for the change. Both one-on-one and group efforts using line supervisors and the guiding coalition members are criti-cal to successful communication of the change vision and strategy.

Stage 5. Empowering Broad-Based Action

Stage five of the change process involves **enabling** others to act in imple-menting the change. Kotter calls this "empowering broad-based action." Many people must be **empowered** to work on implementing the change. In other words, if employees don't have the authority already, they need it to make decisions at their level for implementing the change.

If everything is dependent on getting approval from above, then the change process bogs down and progress comes to a halt. An illustration of how overdependence on approval from above can cause problems is found in both Gulf Wars when the United States invaded Iraq. One of the main reasons the United States was successful so quickly in each war was due to the command structure and speed of decision-making. The Iraq army was steeped in a decision-making model of command and control. Taking the initiative and making decisions without approval from above was not done. In fact, to do so in the Iraq army was to risk severe reprisals, including death.

The opposite was true in the U.S. Army. Personnel from low-ranking officers to noncommissioned officers were encouraged to make on-the-spot decisions as needed in order to achieve the mission. When events changed on the ground, the U.S. Army was able to respond rapidly, where-as the Iraqi army was not.

The U.S. Army took advantage of this difference in the command and control structures by targeting Iraq's communication infrastructure with its first air strikes. Once communications were disrupted, Iraq's personnel had no way to get direction from above. They were unaccustomed to mak-ing decisions without approval. Thus, they were hamstrung in making the necessary military decisions in time to be effective.

Having all the change decisions either made at the top or needing to be approved through a long chain of command is precisely the trap you want to avoid. Avoiding this trap requires empowering employees and their supervisors to make decisions and take actions at their levels within the agency with regard to implementation of the change. The latitude for making these decisions needs definition, and clarifying the sideboards is an important part of effective empowerment. Sideboards can include, for example: Do not exceed your budget, stay within agency policies, stay within politically sensitive boundaries, and so on. What is to be achieved needs to be explained. Then empower employees and hold them accountable. See Chapter One, *Work Plans – A Multifaceted Tool You Can't Do Without* and the Five Rs process of delegation and empowerment described there.

There's another good reason for empowering as many people as possible to help implement a major change. All the decisions made through the levels of the agency regarding implementation cannot be made by only one or a few controlling individuals. It's a matter of practicality. Less obvious but equally important is the fact that not all bosses may buy into the change. I learned up close and personal how this could become a blocking force for change. It was during the first major change I tried to implement for an agency.

The two deputy directors of this agency occupied the number two slots, just under the director. Both deputies gave lip service to the change effort. However, one deputy was not receptive. He reasoned that he had learned to use the old system and would not have the same level of freedom to move funds at his whim under the new system. The only way I was able to overcome this resistance was by empowering the levels of employees under this deputy to implement the change. The deputy could not openly oppose the change efforts of those under him since the director was supportive of the change.

Similar barriers to implementing the change can occur from bosses regardless of their level in the agency's hierarchy. Empowering others is a way to help overcome this. But remember that lower-level employees must have been a noticeable part of the entire process up to this point and have buy-in for empowerment to succeed at this stage.

THE RELUCTANT BOSS

I've found that one of the most agonizing issues that agencies are reluctant to face is the resistant boss who stalls change in his or her part of the agency. Ignoring this problem is a recipe for killing the change process. Others will see that resistance is tolerated and then it spreads like a virus.

One solution is to have a frank discussion with the resistant boss. I suggest beginning the discussion with how important the change is, and then say something like ". . . and here is what I need from you." Then ask, "What will you bring to the effort?" If the boss remains resistant, it should become obvious in this discussion. Remember the axiom that people will change as the agency changes—double meaning intended!

Ken Haddad (pers. comm.) found that reluctant bosses in FWC's change process were very clever in hiding their resistance. Ken held meetings with lower-level employees, excluding their bosses, and asked the employees to tell him if they were being held back. In this manner, Ken was able to discover the hidden resistors and either get them in line or out of the way. This demonstrated to everyone that Ken was serious about implementation. It actually sent a great and very appreciated message to the frontline staff and created a wonderful atmosphere for buy-in.

Some other barriers to change implementation usually can be found in the old ways the agency is organized, its old systems for accomplishing work, and/or the skills previously applied when new skills are needed. Refer to Chapter Two, A *Model of Agency Interdependencies*, to review the Big Six areas that may need some realignment for a new change to successfully become part of the agency.

Stage 6. Celebrate Victories

Stage six of the change process is a stage of celebration and reward. Here you celebrate significant, visible, short-term victories in the agency change process. It's an important stage, easily overlooked, especially in the fish and wildlife culture. Part of our "missionary-like zeal" is the concentration on working for wildlife to the point that once success is achieved, we immediately move on to the next challenge. The challenges are never ending and our mission is of personal importance. We seldom take time to stop and celebrate success. There always appears too much to do. But not planning for and celebrating short-term victories in a change effort is a major mistake!

Why is this so important? As state agencies, we are part of the public process and thus part of the political processes. That means that directors, commissioners, and governors must support, or at least not oppose, the changes sought within an agency. Remember the authority figure's role in any system is to keep order and provide protection and direction. When change-related stress is created in any system, the fallout of appeals to the governor, commissioners, and the agency director from various members of the agency and the public can be intense. Those in authority positions need support in order to resist this pressure and resist immediately "restoring order" by killing the change effort.

Short-term wins are what provide proof of the change progress and the beginnings of positive advancements! Without these wins, authority figures and employees soon tire of the stress of change. In other words, without short-term successes, the longing for the comfort of the old way of doing things soon overcomes any support for the change efforts.

An agency's change process must include a **plan** for these short-term wins! It is not enough to hope that they occur—they may not. Short-term wins require first setting short-term goals and then celebrating their achievement. Kotter (1996) makes a couple of important points regarding these short-term wins:

- Don't succumb to the temptation of manufacturing false wins! People will soon see through this gambit. The resulting loss in credibility can kill the change effort. Your short-term victories must be real!

- The wins must be visible and unquestionably related to the change efforts. They cannot be interpreted as resulting from any other events or actions than those related to the change effort. Resist the temptation to claim a win when it may be due to events other than the change efforts.

- Don't claim victory too soon. It may be tempting to tell everyone, "We have won—the change worked!" But doing so before the change is complete and fully institutionalized leads everyone to stop working on the change effort. Why? Because such news relieves the pressure to keep up change efforts. Change stops short, then the change progress begins to slide backwards as the agency slips back into the comforts of doing things the old way.

CASE EXAMPLE: CLAIMING SUCCESS TOO EARLY

This last point was illustrated well to me in an experience I had several years ago. I had been working with the Association of Fish and Wildlife Agency's Management Assistance Team and we had completed a lengthy review of a natural resource agency where we recommended several significant changes. The publics, the governor, and the legislature in that state were very interested in ensuring that the agency made the recommended changes. Soon after our recommendations were made public, the agency director was replaced with a new person.

This new director was under pressure to make the agency changes recommended. We had let the agency know that, due to the magnitude of the changes and the size of this state agency, it would take several years to complete the changes we had recommended. Imagine our surprise when the new director claimed to have succeeded in making all the changes within nine months of taking office. When we were invited to visit the agency and meet with the new director, he did his best to convince us he had succeeded. It was obvious that this was just bluster and an attempt to look good. In reality, the agency change efforts had ceased and significant change had never occurred. The new director may have achieved his selfish goals of looking good to his superiors and relieving the stress on the agency systems and employees to make changes. But unfortunately, the real long-term result for the agency was killing the effort to improve and instead resuming business as usual!

Stage 7. Consolidating Gains and Keeping Up the Pressure

Stage seven of Kotter's eight-stage process is consolidating gains and keeping up the pressure for change. This can be summarized in the concept of "never let up!" It is very easy by this point in the change process to become worn down with all the effort expended so far. There is a strong desire among many to take a break and rest on the laurels of what has been accomplished so far. Letting up now is a major mistake and the result will likely be ultimate failure of the change effort.

It reminds me of Chief Joseph and the Nez Perce tribe that was being pursued by the U.S. Army in 1877. The tribe successfully fought several battles with the army and eluded capture while traveling over 1,000 miles across Idaho, Wyoming, and Montana in an effort to escape to Canada and avoid relocation to a reservation. The Nez Perce, travel weary, starving, cold, and suffering from their ordeal, arrived at the Bears Paw Mountains of Montana and could see Canada only forty miles away across the open prairie. They stopped for the night in order to let the women and children rest. All the weary tribal travelers anticipated crossing the Canadian boundary the next day. During the night, however, Colonel Nelson Miles and General Oliver Howard were able to move troops close to the camp, and the next morning at daybreak, after a short battle, they captured many of the Nez Perce and returned them to a reservation. The Nez Perce were so close.

While change efforts may not encompass the life-and-death results of the battle of the Bears Paw Mountains, the point is that stopping short, even when success seems within grasp, can lead to failure of your change effort. Never underestimate the power of the years of old ways of doing things. Even though these old ways may currently be dormant, stopping the change effort to rest and recuperate from the stress can allow the old ways to resurface and lead to eventual failure of your change effort.

Stage 8. Anchor the Change in the Culture

The eighth and last stage in Kotter's change process is that of anchoring new approaches in the culture. It is about making sure the old ways of doing business don't resurface to oust the new change in place. This is perhaps the most important stage to overall success when implementing change!

Kotter's uses an analogy of plants and root systems to illustrate anchoring change in the culture, and this is very fitting for a natural resource agency. Making a major change in an agency can be likened to cutting down the existing plants on a piece of land. Since part of my experience included work in Texas, the old existing plants might be considered as South Texas brush such as mesquite, blackbrush, brasil, and other thorny plants. Agency change is like cutting down the brush and planting a new species such as buffelgrass. When the change is in place, the buffelgrass has become established overlaying the previously brush-covered land. At this point, many would consider the job of achieving the change done. This is a mistake!

If you stop watering and nurturing the buffelgrass, the brush reasserts itself and shades out the grass, eventually reclaiming the land. This happens because the old root systems of the brush plants are mature and run deep from years of establishment, just like the old ways of doing things in an agency are deeply rooted in years of employees' experiences. If the new change in place is not nurtured and the old ways continually pruned back, then the new change will not last. It often takes a number of years for the new "roots" of the change to grow and mature in the agency culture before it will permanently replace the old ways of doing things. I usually advise agencies to expect about five years to pass before a major change effort can be fully institutionalized.

Change efforts in wildlife agencies can be established and then disappear. I have observed many agencies make major efforts to implement needed changes that resulted in a waste of time and resources. In some other agencies, the director implemented internal changes that included restructuring, new programs, and shifting of resources only to have everything revert back to the way it was as soon as the director left the agency. Don't underestimate the importance of **anchoring** the change in the agency culture if you want it to last!

Summary

Major change in agencies is never easy. But change is necessary for improving and for responding to changing conditions. Refusing to change leads to stagnation and eventual irrelevance as a public agency. Accepting the challenge means facing many obstacles, not the least of which is determining **when** change is needed. Determining when change should be made is a strategic decision that is seldom certain. Understanding the U Curve concepts can be helpful in making this strategic leap. Realize that experimentation will be needed and failures are to be expected when seeking a new path.

There are eight stages of change that must be implemented in order to stand the best chance for success. These eight stages are:

1.   Establishing a sense of urgency.
2.   Creating the guiding coalition.
3.   Developing a vision and strategy.
4.   Communicating the change vision.
5.   Empowering broad-based action.
6.   Generating short-term wins.
7.   Consolidating gains and producing more change.
8.   Anchoring new approaches in the culture.

Taking on the task of leading change requires a strong commitment to the agency's future, especially because success is not guaranteed. Be encouraged though—I have seen first-hand successful change in the Montana Department of Fish, Wildlife & Parks that I worked for over twenty-five years ago, in the Florida Wildlife Commission, in the Nevada Division of Wildlife, and in numerous other state agencies. It can be done! What you have read in this chapter can help you. More important, it takes courage and commitment as well as strong leadership, which is the subject of the next chapter.

Literature Cited

Collins, Jim. 2001. *Good to Great*. Harper Collins Publishers. New York, NY. 300 pp.

Covey, Steven M. R. 2006. *The Speed of Trust*. Simon and Schuster, Inc. New York, NY. 354 pp.

Covey, Steven R. 1989. *The Seven Habits of Highly Effective People*. Simon and Schuster, Inc. New York, NY. 358 pp.

Duck, Jeanie D. 1993. "Managing Change: The Art of Balancing." *Harvard Business Review*. Nov.–Dec. Harvard Business School Press. Boston, MA.

Gino, Francesca and Bradley Staats. 2015. "Why Organizations Don't Learn." *Harvard Business Review*. Nov.–Dec. Harvard Business School Press. Boston, MA.

Goss, Tracy, Richard Pascal, and Anthony Athos. 1993. "The Reinvention Roller Coaster: Risking the Present for a Powerful Future. *Harvard Business Review*. Nov.–Dec. Harvard Business School Press. Boston, MA.

Greiner, Larry, Thomas Cummings, and Arvind Bharbri. 2003. "When New CEOs Succeed and Fail: 4-D Theory of Strategic Transformation." *Organizational Dynamics*. 32 (3), pp. 1-17.

Grove, Andrew S. 1999. *Only the Paranoid Survive*. Doubleday. New York, NY. 224 pp.

Kennedy, J. J. (1985). "Viewing Wildlife Managers as a Unique Professional Culture." *The Wildlife Society Bulletin*. 13 (4), pp. 571-579.

Jacobsen, Cynthia A. 2008. "Wildlife Conservation and Management in the 21st Century: Understanding Challenges for Institutional Transformation. Ph.D. Dis. Cornell Univ. Ithaca, NY. 146 pp.

Kotter, John. 2012. "How the Most Innovative Companies Capitalize on Today's Rapid-Fire Strategic Challenges—and Still Make Their Numbers." *Harvard Business Review*. Boston, MA. Nov. pp. 44-58.

Kotter, John. 2008. A *Sense of Urgency*. Harvard Business School Press. Boston, MA. 196 pp.

Kotter, John. 1996. *Leading Change*. Harvard Business School Press. Boston, MA. 187 pp.

Lawler III, Edward and Christopher Worley. 2006. *Built to Change*. Jossey-Bass, San Francisco, CA. 334 pp.

Machiavelli, Niccolo. 2003. *The Prince*. Bantam Books. New York, NY. 166 pp.

Martin, Roger. 1993. "Changing the Mind of the Corporation." *Harvard Business Review*. Nov.-Dec. Harvard Business School Press. Boston, MA.

Maslow, Abraham. 1943. "A Theory of Human Motivation." *Psychological Review*. Amer. Psychol. Assoc. Washington, DC.

Minter, Richard and Scott McEwen. 2014. *Eyes on Target: Inside Stories from the Brotherhood of the U.S. Navy SEALS*. Hachette Book Group. New York, NY.

Roosevelt, Franklin D. 1938. "Address at Oglethorpe University." Reprinted in *The Public Papers and Addresses of Franklin D. Roosevelt 1928–32*, Vol. 1. Random House. New York, NY. 639 pp.

CHAPTER FIVE

Leadership

Before deciding to take on a leadership role, brace yourself for a sobering interpretation of what leadership is, what it requires, and the dangers involved.

In my work with state fish and wildlife agencies, I frequently hear agency directors or division chiefs referred to as "leaders." But no one really gives use of the word leader much thought. The term leader can be vague and confusing, meaning a plethora of different things to different people. During my twenty-five years working with state fish and wildlife agencies, I've seen agency people in high positions of authority who provided great leadership. I've also seen others with similar levels of authority provide the worst experiences possible.

Appointments to Positions of Authority

Often appointments of new agency directors, wildlife commissioners, or others in state government follow the flow of political currents and elections of new governors. While we all hope political appointments provide capable and good leaders, the outcome is far from guaranteed. Political appointments are often based on friendship, loyalty, political favors, and political party considerations—factors that often overshadow appointees' managerial, administrative, or, most importantly, leadership skills. Such skills are often considered a side benefit after other considerations are met.

The main qualities sought in candidates often seem to be loyalty to the appointing power and a willingness to solve problems and provide order within state government. Solving problems and providing order for an agency, for example, requires good administration but that is not leadership! To explain this statement, let's look at the definition of leadership more closely. How have we historically thought about leadership, and how does leadership differ from authority? How does leadership relate to purpose, and what are the risks associated with leadership?

Historical Development of Leadership Theory

Historically, the study of leadership has taken many different paths. Thomas Carlyle wrote about leadership in his 1841 book *On Heroes, Hero-Worship, and the Heroic in History*. His view was that history was the story of great men and their impacts on societies. A later leadership theory, commonly referred to as **trait theory,** assumed that great leaders possessed certain traits of personality and character that made them leaders. Scientific studies of this approach however, have been unable to define any such set of traits. A resurgence of this theory occurred in the 1980s when Dr. David Campbell at the Center for Creative Leadership in Denver, Colorado, developed the Campbell Leadership Index, which uses self and associates' scores to rate an individual on a set of twenty-one "leadership traits." There appear to be some correlations between this set of traits and the people assessed to be leaders by their peers (Guynn 1999). Nevertheless, the majority of statistical evidence is not encouraging for this approach to leadership.

Another theory, **situational leadership,** posits that leaders are a result of their time and positioning at the juncture of powerful political and social forces. This theory, as posed by Herbert Spencer in 1884, suggests that the times in which a person lives make the leader.

In the 1950s, theorists began to combine the situational approach with the trait approach and developed what is referred to as the **contingency model** to explain leadership. This model suggests that the appropriate style of leadership and the traits used to lead should both vary depending on the requirements of each particular situation. More recently, this approach has become known as **situational leadership.** Paul Hersey (1985) and Ken Blanchard (2010) have written extensively about this model. Next came the **transactional model,** where theorists postulated that the interactions between leaders and followers (transactions) were primary in allowing one person to gain and maintain influence over others (Bass 2008).

Much of the research of leadership seems to be directed at studies of military figures and their accomplishments. Let's take a closer look at the military emphasis since most law enforcement programs in state wildlife agencies are based upon the military rank and structure. The military concept of leadership emphasizes creating followership! Dwight Eisenhower is famous for his demonstration of leadership using a piece of rope. When the rope is pushed from the back then the rope does not move forward but just folds upon itself. However, when pulled from the front, then the rope follows in the desired direction and makes straightforward progress. The point Eisenhower made is that in military situations it is important to lead from the front of the battle line.

The military system relies heavily on creating a system or environment to encourage followership. Creating this followership environment is done through many practices:

- Breaking down individualism through emphasizing all having the same uniform, haircut, etc.
- Emphasis on becoming part of a group (squad, platoon, company, etc.).
- Officers are separated from enlisted (different quarters, dining area, etc.) to emphasize officers as authority figures and obedience to commands without question.
- Officers are expected to set the example and make decisions for those following them.
- Support for your buddies and each other as part of the group is emphasized to the point that soldiers in battle report that they are primarily fighting for their buddies safety and respect rather than for the flag, or some principle.

This military emphasis of leadership based upon followership is interesting, but I believe it's incomplete. Heifetz (1994) points out that not only the military model but also all the previously mentioned theories of leadership are all based on influence or control. Heifetz recommends adding criteria first suggested by James MacGregor Burns (1978). Burns suggested that leadership should accomplish two things: 1) socially useful goals, and 2) elevation of followers to a higher moral level. Heifetz applies Burns' idea by recommending that any definition of leadership should take into account **values** and **results** in addition to influence. This concept then gets us away from just influencing followers and focuses on what is accomplished by those being led.

Adolph Hitler would be considered a great "leader" when using only the criteria of influence over others, yet few would describe the Holocaust as a sign of great leadership. A man like George Armstrong Custer leading others to their deaths at the Little Bighorn is one of the strongest signs of influence over others, but it fails James MacGregor Burns' and Heifetz's definition of leadership. At a more localized level, many of us can think of political figures that had followers but who were very disappointing in what they accomplished during their administrations. Thus, for the purposes of this chapter, I will define leadership as **not only influence over others but also influencing others to accomplish socially useful goals.**

Leadership and Authority

How does this definition then relate to being in a position of authority? Often the names of great leaders are synonymous with people who have or had great authority. Abraham Lincoln, Dwight Eisenhower, General George Patton, Teddy Roosevelt, John Kennedy, and Margaret Thatcher are often mentioned in discussions of leadership. But what about people like Gandhi? He led India's search for successful self-government following the end of British colonialism. Gandhi never held a political office, so his authority level was small, but his leadership was undeniable. Martin Luther King, Jr., considered one of the great leaders of our civil rights movement, was a Southern Baptist minister without any political position. South Africa's Nelson Mandela is a similar figure. He influenced the end of Apartheid while spending twenty-seven years in prison. Clearly, people can carry out leadership regardless of any positions of authority.

There are pros and cons to having authority and providing leadership. Those in positions of authority can more easily get the attention of people. Those with authority have greater access to information from a broader array of sources. However, those with positions of authority seldom have the luxury of devoting all their time to one issue.

Those without authority have the ability to focus on only one issue and they have a more narrow but frontline, detailed view of the issue. The other advantage of leading without authority is that you are seldom expected to provide the answer to the issue and can focus people's attention on working toward mutual solutions. In contrast, authority figures are often expected to provide the answer to the issue.

The view that leadership is completely independent of positional authority is a significant conceptual departure from the traditional view of leadership. If we accept that leadership is independent of a person's position in an organization, or society, then it follows that the exercise of authority is not the same as the exercise of leadership—in other words, the fact that you have a fancy job title is no indication of leadership! Why is it then that so many people in authority positions are referred to as leaders? To understand this, we must first look at the exercise of authority. In its simplest form, authority is the exercise of influence over others by virtue of position in a hierarchy. This position in organizations is bestowed by the organization (through hiring or promotion), or it's bestowed from powers outside and above the organization (like commissions and/or political appointments). As already discussed, bestowing of a position from which to influence others is not a guarantee that leadership will be exercised. In fact, the opposite is often the case.

The Unspoken Contract

One of the reasons that actual leadership is difficult for authority figures is due to the "unspoken contract" (Linsky pers. comm.) between the person upon which a position of authority is bestowed and those bestowing the position. The powers bestowing a position of authority usually desire the person receiving the position to achieve a long litany of things. These desires may change with the position and with the bestowing powers. But a commonality exists in that all the desires of those bestowing power can be categorized into three groups. The groups are:

Protection - The person upon whom authority is bestowed is expected to provide protection of or defend the powers doing the bestowing and the people and resources assigned to the authority.

Order - The authority figure is expected to provide order for the subordinates carrying out intended tasks. In other words quell disagreements, solve problems, and keep things running smoothly.

Direction - The authority figure is expected to provide direction to subordinates by giving them goals and objectives to be accomplished and to move the organization along a well-defined, desired path.

Those reporting to the authority figure—the followers or subordinates—also hold these same three kinds of expectations of their authority figure. These people look to their authority figure to protect them and their jobs, provide safety and order in the workplace, and provide direction for the organization and their work.

An authority figure who fails to meet these expectations for either the powers above them or for their subordinates does so at his or her own peril. It is easy to see that if you disappoint those above you in an organization, it can lead to having your authority taken away through a variety of means including being fired or demoted. But disappointing your subordinates can have equally dire consequences. For example, if all your employees were to sign a petition asking for your removal, or refuse to work as long as you were their supervisor, then your deauthorization (firing or removal from current position) is essentially guaranteed. The higher positions of authority in modern American society are elected positions. Here too, we see the story of deauthorization play out when politicians disappoint their constituents and are voted out of office or even impeached.

The burden of authority lies in the unspoken contract of the authority figure to meet the expectations of providing protection, order, and direction. Meeting these expectations is good and noble work; it's just not leadership! (Linsky pers. comm.) Rather it's good administration. Administration is the daily stuff that makes organizations and society in general run smoothly. This is a very important and desired component of any authority contract, but leadership is concerned with something altogether different.

Leadership is about Adaptation

Darwin developed the concept of evolution—animals adapting to changes in their environment. Animals adapt by mutation and changes in their genetic code. Individual humans, societies, and organizations adapt by learning. The solution to issues where beliefs and values are in conflict can only be achieved if the people involved learn and adapt. Hence, we use the term *adaptive leadership*. It is about change. The road of evolution is strewn with the bones of species that failed to adapt. I might add that the bones of organizations that fail to change also litter the path of organizational evolution.

Adaptive leadership means **changing** things from their current state to a different and better state. Good administration means meeting expectations and keeping things running smoothly. Thus, the administrative goal of making the current state of the organization operate smoothly is almost always contrary to the goal of change with its resulting disruptions and angst.

An example is the change wrought by Theodore Roosevelt regarding America's view of its natural resources. The change from a pervasive view of using natural resources only for human benefit and profit to a view of conserving natural resources for future generations (and for their own sake) was a major shift in thinking for American society. Roosevelt faced major opposition from business and industry when he set aside such areas as the Grand Canyon and protected it from mining. Congress sought to control Roosevelt's conservation actions through legislation. It caused Roosevelt to rely often on his executive authority to implement programs that would have been rejected by the traditionalist forces that controlled Congress. In another example, the civil rights changes led by Martin Luther King, Jr. did not come without significant angst and disruption of the normal order for American society. This lack of order was evidenced by riots, killing of civil rights workers, and other disruptions concurrent with the change.

The Fear Associated with Change

There is great fear and opposition associated with change because major change incorporates the potential for loss and people naturally resist loss! John Kotter (1996) cites this as the reason for great complacency in organizations contemplating major change. Even if the change has the potential to foster a much better organization and better performance, there are still fears, such as:

I may not be able to do the new tasks required of me as effectively as the tasks I already know.

My job may not be as important in the new, changed organization.

I'm more comfortable with the devil I know (problems in the current organization) than the devil I don't know.

Successfully bringing about change entails making people uncomfortable. It means not keeping things running smoothly but creating stress and actually disappointing subordinates and superiors in one or more of their expectations for protection, order, and direction. The risk is great and there are limits to how uncomfortable you can make others without their deauthorizing you. It's a matter of making people uncomfortable, but at a rate they can stand.

Unfortunately, the limits to which you can push people to address change in any situation are unknown. They vary for each individual and each group. The people and groups themselves cannot tell you what their limit is until they experience it. The person exercising leadership has to improvise and read people's reactions as the progress on change unfolds. This requires constant attention and adjustment in leadership actions. You are regulating the pressure on the individuals and groups involved in the change. The goal of leadership is to keep the pressure high enough to overcome complacency, but not so high that the person leading the change gets deauthorized.

Leadership is Risky

This is why you so seldom see leadership at high levels of authority—it's risky, and if you have climbed to the top of an organization you have even more to lose. It's much safer to be a good administrator and meet everyone's expectations as fully as possible than to be a leader for change.

Examples of leadership risks abound. Can you think of someone considered to be a great leader who met with tragic consequences? Maybe Abraham Lincoln, John F. Kennedy, or Martin Luther King, Jr. comes to mind. All were assassinated. Nelson Mandela, who lead the change to end apartheid in South Africa, spent twenty-seven years in prison, and many lesser-known people who exercised leadership for change suffered demotions, ostracism, and reprimands. Those in positions of authority often seek to restore order rather than allow a degree of disorder concurrent with making a major change.

There Must be Purpose

If leadership is so hazardous, then why would anyone want to take leadership actions? The answer is because of commitment to a purpose. Ideals and purposes that we hold dear are what cause us to be willing to take the risks of leading major change. Without purpose, then the fears of demotion, job loss, ostracism, or even assassination overcome any willingness to take risks.

Leadership is an Activity

Often when discussing leadership it is easier to discuss people who are generally seen as great leaders. Consider the terms marksmanship, woodsmanship, horsemanship, and leadership. We don't identify marksmanship as a person, or woodsmanship as a person, the same for horsemanship. We think of those as activities that a person performs with a degree of skill. When a person performs those activities with skill, we call them a marksman, woodsman, or horseman. The same should hold true for the term leadership. It is not a person but a set of activities.

Leadership is all about taking actions to influence others to achieve change for a socially useful purpose and also elevate people to a higher moral level. It is something you do! Leadership then is better described as an **activity** and not as a person. The experts at Cambridge Leadership Associates (Hugh O'Doherty pers. comm.) encourage dropping altogether the term "leader" from our vocabulary. Leadership can be done by anyone. **It is an activity done by some people some of the time but not by anyone all the time.** In other words, leadership is a choice, while authority is bestowed.

If leadership is different from authority, then we are back to the question, "why are authority figures frequently referred to as leaders?" Remember that most people in an organization or management system fear change and want their authority figure to keep order and lessen stress. Calling the authority figure a leader is a way to seductively bribe them to keep on just doing good administration while creating no major change.

Two Types of Issues

Those in authority positions are expected to resolve issues facing their organization and its constituents. This is part of the "unspoken contract." Those in authority positions are required to deal with two basic categories of issues. The confusing part is that dealing with one category of issues is just good administrative work, but dealing with the second category of issues it is actually leadership. Sound confusing?

Four Case Examples

Let's first look at the two basic kinds of issues by considering four real examples from the headlines of state fish and wildlife agency activities. Then we'll explore the differences and similarities of the issues. Identifying the type of issue you're facing is the first step to its successful resolution. Issues of one type shown below will require using good **administrative** skills, while the other type of issue in the examples below will require engaging in **leadership** activities.

Case Example 1: Montana's Hunting Access on Private Lands

CONTEXT:

Much of the western United States is blessed with large amounts of public lands. Hunters enjoy the unhampered use of these lands for recreation much of the year. Historically, the private lands of the West were often open to hunting just by asking permission. However, the closure of private lands has increased over time (Rounds 1975, Guynn 1979, Dickson 2014). These closures are a source of heated debate throughout much of the West. In Montana, the issue regarding access to Montana private lands by resident hunters was a recurring one.

THE HUNTERS' VIEW:

The squeeze of declining access to private lands had been tightening for some time. Hunters were feeling the pinch! They blamed outfitters in the state as part of the problem because outfitters were continually leasing more private lands for their clients. The concept of wildlife as a public resource was being challenged by the exercise of private property rights to lease and close private lands to public hunting even though those lands harbored numerous species of publicly owned wildlife.

THE LANDOWNERS' VIEW:
Landowners who were leasing and closing their lands to public hunting felt justified in their actions; their values regarding private property rights were deeply entrenched. No government entity was going to strip them of their rights as landowners! After all, the landowners felt that they "fed" the elk and deer all year long and deserved something for it.

THE OUTFITTERS' VIEW
Outfitters thought the Montana Department of Fish, Wildlife & Parks (FWP) was curbing private enterprise and personal businesses because the agency required nonresident hunters to draw for a license in a lottery-style system. The rights of private enterprise to engage in legal business should not be interfered with by government! The western values of letting people engage freely in business were being trampled by FWP.

This issue involving private lands and public wildlife was constantly cropping up in the state legislature. Finally it came to a head in 1993 when twelve different bills were introduced into the Montana Legislature, each bill dealt with a different facet of the issue. The legislature debated the bills and soon realized that none of the different interest groups involved in the problem had talked to one another and all the bills conflicted. The legislature declined to pass any of the twelve bills introduced and instead passed a joint resolution between the house and the senate asking the governor to appoint a blue-ribbon panel to deal with the issue. Of course the governor, seeing this was a wildlife issue, passed the burden of solving the issue onto FWP (Guynn 1997).

FWP had several options. The agency could try to get all the interested parties involved and facilitate these parties working out some kind of solution as yet undetermined, or FWP could be decisive and make some hard choices to "solve" the issue by the way it chose to issue permits and set seasons, etc.

FWP had the legal authority to make regulations and affect the problem in various ways. Many of the contentious factions wanted FWP to solve the problem for them. Of course, which solution was "right" depended on which faction you talked to. FWP could choose to be decisive and, while not pleasing everyone, could "solve" the issue. The option of opening the problem to all the factions involved and trying to referee for a decision was an untraveled path through unknown territory. Would you call this an adaptive leadership issue or an administrative issue? What would you or your agency do to solve this?

Case Example 2: South Dakota's East Versus West Situation

Let's look at an issue that occurred in South Dakota that had many similarities with the Montana issue. I am indebted to John Cooper, former director of South Dakota Game, Fish and Parks (SD GF&P) for this example. To understand the problem in South Dakota it is important to know some of the specifics of that state. Essentially there is a big difference between eastern South Dakota (east of the Missouri River) and western South Dakota (west of the Missouri River). These areas are locally referred to as East River and West River. East River is more agricultural, with grain crops and a high pheasant population. It's responsible for the reputation of South Dakota as a great pheasant state. Lots of nonresident hunters journey to that part of South Dakota each year to pursue the colorful birds. These hunters bring in a lot of cash to the state and are important to landowners as a source of income after their fields are harvested.

West River is more rangeland than farmland. The drier climate in that part of the state makes farming there less tenable. It's open country broken by hills and draws and is home to both mule deer and white-tailed deer. The open prairie also harbors good numbers of pronghorn. Large blocks of private lands interspersed with "checkerboard" public sections make up most of the ranches. It's more big-game country than pheasant country. The big-game populations attract nonresident hunters who've succeeded at drawing a valid license through SD GF&P's lottery system.

WESTERN RIVER LANDOWNERS' VIEW

The West River landowners saw the issue as one of unfairness: they were more restricted from making money by leasing hunting for big game, while their East River brethren were able to make significant income from pheasant hunters. The problem as identified by the West River landowners was that nonresident pheasant hunters did not have to draw for a license and came to the state in large numbers. The big-game hunters had to draw for a license; therefore, the landowners seeking to serve this clientele had no way of knowing if their prospective customers would get a license. Hunters a landowner had booked for a hunt had no guarantee of drawing a license. The West River landowners viewed building a big-game hunting business under these circumstances as hit or miss due to SD GF&P's imposed lottery for big-game licenses.

The West River landowners felt the state was infringing on their rights to lease hunting or charge hunters for access. More specifically, it was SD GF&P that was infringing. The landowners recognized that SD GF&P needed to limit licenses dependent upon the size of the game populations. They saw the solution as SD GF&P issuing licenses to the landowners who could then resell them. This would allow SD GF&P to control hunter numbers and allow landowners to control who got licenses and build hunting businesses on their ranches.

The other stakeholder group in this problem was the resident hunters in South Dakota. Inherent was a strong value of wildlife being available equally to all (through a lottery, etc.), and the idea that hunting should not be limited to just those who were willing to pay a landowner, that is, hunting available only to the rich. This value is part of the North American model of wildlife conservation that is a deeply held concept for sportsmen and wildlife management agencies (Prukop and Regan 2005). This model can be found in the literature of such organizations as the Rocky Mountain Elk Foundation, Boone and Crockett Club, The Wildlife Society, and others. Wildlife being equally available to all, regardless of social or economic status, was supported by the SD GF&P through the laws that had always listed hunting licenses as nontransferable. In other words, no one could get a license and then give or sell it to someone else.

This issue of landowner rights, equal ability to gain licenses, and hunting as a business, became a major hot potato for SD GF&P when a group of West River landowners got the ear of the South Dakota governor. They made their case for SD GP&P selling big-game licenses to landowners as transferrable licenses. This would mean landowners could then turn around and sell (transfer) the licenses to hunters of their choice. But, as mentioned previously, SD GF&P had a history of regulations prohibiting transferrable licenses. The agency could change that and make licenses transferrable as the governor wished, or it could stand its ground and defy the governor.

Another option was to involve the different stakeholders in some sort of citizen participation process and try to work out a solution that might be mutually agreeable or not. There appeared to be no way to win on this one for SD GF&P. Would you call this an adaptive leadership issue or an administrative issue? What would you or your agency do to solve this?

Case Example 3: Polluting Montana's Trout River

The third issue was one that occurred as a big surprise to Montana's Department of Fish, Wildlife & Parks (FWP). The state had mandated that all agencies remove underground gasoline storage tanks over a period of years. This was a way to ensure against rust and leakage of gasoline into soils and water supplies. FWP was following a schedule to remove underground storage tanks and replace them with aboveground storage. When it came time to replace the underground gasoline storage tank at an FWP site in Livingston, Montana, a major surprise awaited. The FWP gasoline storage tank in Livingston was beside the Yellowstone River. Excavation of the underground tank revealed it had actually been leaking! There was gasoline soaking into the ground and potentially affecting one of the state's and the nation's blue-ribbon trout streams, the fabled Yellowstone River.

It was a sensitive problem. FWP was charged with managing and protecting trout streams, yet the agency was actually causing potential damage. The town of Livingston was a central gathering point for anglers fishing on the Yellowstone. Local businesses were dependent on tourist and angler income for a significant part of their annual cash flow. FWP was red-faced and guilty. Would you call this an adaptive leadership issue or an administrative issue? What would you or your agency do?

Case Example 4: Waterfowl Disease Outbreak

The fourth issue deals with an outbreak of avian botulism on a reservoir where waterfowl had been concentrating. The reservoir was adjacent to a major urban area, and dead ducks, geese, and shorebirds were littering the shoreline. The local newspaper had carried a story about the numerous dead and dying birds. The local Audubon chapter and SPCA had sent members to the shoreline to rescue sick birds. The public outcry was for the state fish and wildlife agency to "do something." It appeared that the agency needed to take charge of the problem and provide a solution. Would you call this an adaptive leadership issue or an administrative issue? What would you or your agency do?

Similarities and Differences of the Four Examples

The previous examples represent many common issues that plague state wildlife agencies. The subjects and the stakeholders may differ, but many commonalities exist. The solutions to each issue may vary, but we can categorize issues as either 1) *adaptive challenges* requiring adaptive leadership actions or 2) *technical problems* requiring good administration. Failing to identify the type of problem you're dealing with is a serious error. Ron Heifetz, et al., (2009) states: "The most common cause of failure in leadership is produced by treating adaptive challenges as if they were technical problems." So what's the definition of an adaptive challenge and how is it different from a technical problem? Let's address the easy one first—technical problems.

TECHNICAL PROBLEMS
These types of problems are familiar to all of us. They share a number of features.

- They have a known solution (they have been solved before)
- There is an accepted process for solving these problems
- They have recognized experts
- They have known roles for those involved in their solution
- There are no conflicts of strongly held values and beliefs between stakeholder groups

A good example of a technical problem is the gasoline leak in the tank along Montana's Yellowstone River. This was a major issue on a national blue-ribbon trout stream, but it was technical in nature. Cleaning up gasoline leaks and solving the problem was expensive and it was highly important to the public. However, there were established procedures for how to do it, experts could be called upon, and it had been solved elsewhere by others. FWP knew what to do. There were no conflicting values between stakeholder groups. The director of the agency needed only to do good administrative work to engage the experts and arrange for the big job of successfully cleaning up the leak.

The disease outbreak in a waterfowl population on a reservoir is another example of a technical problem. There were known procedures for collection and necropsy of the animals and testing for the presence of disease. Also, there were known solutions for how to treat various diseases. There were experts in avian diseases, and defined roles for who does what, how, and when—field staff collect specimens, disease experts do the lab work, and so on. Everyone involved agreed on the need to solve the problem, and there were no strong conflicting values and beliefs regarding the issue. Only good administration was required to engage the experts in their roles and to arrange for the work to be implemented.

Another example of a technical problem is a game warden making an arrest. It's technical in that there are specific arrest procedures, an expert (the warden), a history exists of having arrested people before, and there are roles for everyone involved in the problem. There's the warden's role, the lawyer's role, the prosecutor's role, and the judge's role. Each is specific in solving the problem. There is no strong conflict of values and beliefs among significant segments of the public regarding the game laws and their enforcement. The solution just needs to be applied using appropriate, time-tested methods.

ADAPTIVE CHALLENGES
Contrast those kinds of problems with the issue in the first example: access to public wildlife on private lands. There were three major groups involved in the controversy: 1) the outfitters and guides within the state, 2) resident sportsmen, and 3) private landowners. Each group had its own set of strongly held values and beliefs that conflicted with the other groups (Guynn 1997).

It was a thorny problem with years of conflict behind it. There were no processes proven successful for solving it, there were no generally accepted experts, there was no foreseeable solution, and no set roles for those involved. The bottom line—FWP had no ready answers. Good administration alone would not solve this. It would require adaptive leadership actions.

Montana's access to public wildlife on private lands was an issue that called for an entirely different approach than the gasoline leak. This type of problem was an example of what Ron Heifetz (2009) calls an adaptive challenge. Adaptive challenges share a common set of characteristics:

- There is no precedent of a known solution (they have not been successfully solved before)
- There is no generally accepted process for solving these problems
- They have no generally recognized experts
- They have no known roles for those involved in their solution
- There are strong conflicts of values and beliefs between stakeholder groups.

The example in South Dakota with ranchers in the western part of the state promoting legislation to make big-game hunting licenses transferrable is another example of an adaptive challenge. There were no accepted experts on what was the "right" answer. There were no generally accepted roles for the stakeholders in solving the problem. And there was no single process guaranteed to solve the issue. In addition, there were strong conflicts of values and beliefs between stakeholder groups. Good administration alone would not suffice. Adaptive leadership was required.

Additional examples of adaptive challenges might include such issues as user conflicts in fish and wildlife, for example, anglers in conflict over using either bait or artificial lures, and hunters in disagreement over archery hunting regulations versus rifle hunting regulations. Again, check the criteria for adaptive issues: no set procedures for solution, have generally not been solved well in the past and continue to crop up, no proven answers, no generally recognized experts at solving these issues, no established roles for those involved in trying to solve the problems, and strongly held values and beliefs that conflict between stakeholder groups.

A primary distinction between technical problems and adaptive challenges is that technical problems usually do not have deeply held values and beliefs in conflict. All those involved in the gasoline leak and the disease outbreak had similar values of wanting to save the river from harm or protect the waterfowl from disease. However, **the nature of adaptive challenges is that they involve stakeholder groups with conflicting values and beliefs.**

It's a mistake to try to use technical fixes on adaptive challenges! But I see this on a regular basis. One agency attempts to solve controversy over wolf reintroductions and management of wolf populations by using only regulatory and biological means. It's a fact that wildlife agencies know how to make regulations, and the biology of wolves is well documented. But attempting to use these logical, technical sources of information as the entire solution does not work when the issue really is about the different deeply held values between the stakeholders.

Sometimes agencies try to transform themselves to appeal to a large percent of the state's citizens that are non-consumptive wildlife users. Agency mandates are made, programs initiated, and budgets changed to fund the new direction. These efforts can fail miserably, however, because making mandates, initiating programs, and changing budget priorities are technically easy steps to take, but they don't address the **values factor.** Changes in the deeply held values of agency employees and traditional stakeholders are necessary to gain the traction for changes in **behaviors** and **practices** required to make the transformation effective.

Deeply held values, beliefs, and practices reside viscerally in our heart and our gut. You simply can't use logic and data alone to effect changes that are emotionally based! It's no wonder that our technical fixes don't work on adaptive issues. Emotional controversy continues in the face of all our logic and data.

It's easy to make the mistake of applying technical fixes to adaptive issues, especially if we don't understand the differences between the two types of issues. Decisions are further complicated by the fact that most issues are composed of multiple parts, some of which are technical and some of which are adaptive. It's the role of the person trying to lead a group in problem solving to tease out the adaptive components of an issue and address them differently than the technical components.

Once the technical aspects have been separated from the adaptive parts of an issue, the technical portion can be solved rather easily because known solutions exist and can be applied. The more difficult part is addressing the issues that are adaptive in nature. Their solutions are not so simple. Solving adaptive issues is usually more time consuming and more difficult than applying technical fixes. Perhaps this is why technical fixes are so appealing even though they don't solve adaptive problems.

Case Example: Bison Controversy in Montana

A good example of a problem with both technical and adaptive components can be found in the bison controversy in Montana during the winter of 1988-1989. I worked for the Montana FWP at the time and saw firsthand the agency struggle with the issue.

BACKGROUND

Wild bison reside in Yellowstone National Park (YNP) on the southern border of Montana. Bison also carry the disease brucellosis. About one-half of the bison in Yellowstone National Park test positive for brucellosis (APHIS 2012). Brucellosis is a disease that causes domestic cattle to abort their calves. It has been eradicated from cattle in many states and those states are certified as brucellosis-free. A state with this certification can allow ranchers to transport and ship cattle with fewer restrictions and health inspections required. That's a major financial plus for ranchers.

Montana is a certified brucellosis-free state and ranchers didn't want an outbreak of brucellosis in any cattle herd, which could cause loss of their statewide brucellosis-free certification.

THE ISSUE

When winter snows build up inside YNP during the winter, bison migrate outside the park and move down the Yellowstone River Valley onto lower-elevation private lands where there is less snow. It's also where ranchers keep their cattle. Ranchers were greatly concerned that the bison would transfer brucellosis to private cattle herds. Ranchers took the position that the bison coming out of the park must be controlled (killed) and not allowed to enter private lands. Herding the bison was attempted without success.

There were many groups across the nation that did not agree with killing YNP bison that left the park's sanctuary. Some adamantly opposed any killing of bison.

Some of the **technical** parts of the issue were:

- Montana FWP and the National Park Service (NPS) surveys documented how many bison were in the park and about how many left the park and when.
- FWP and NPS had data on how many bison tested positive for brucellosis.
- There was experience and data on the ineffectiveness of herding bison.
- Many Montana hunters voiced a desire for the opportunity to hunt bison.
- Data from Texas A&M researchers showed that brucellosis could be transferred from bison to cattle, at least in a situation where the animals were penned up together.
- There was past experience in how to use hunters to kill bison.
- There was no practical way to vaccinate all the bison in the park.

Using the technical issues and the facts, the answer was clearly just to call in hunters and shoot bison as they left the park. This would eliminate the threat of brucellosis, please hunters, and appease the ranchers. However, it would also infuriate the many other people in Montana and across the nation who did not want to see the bison killed.

Some of the **adaptive** parts of the issue were:

- Some groups saw this main problem as a slaughter of "their" park bison and opposed the state taking such measures. Their core belief was that national park bison belonged to everyone in the United States and that a few locals in Montana should not be able to dictate the killing of a national treasure and an American icon.
- Some groups saw this as an anti-hunting issue and believed that banning hunting for bison was a step toward further banning of all hunting.
- Other groups believed that humans should not interfere; let nature take its course with the bison's' natural winter migration.
- Ranchers saw the federal government's encroaching on and threatening their livelihood by maintaining on parklands bison that would come onto private property. Basically, the value at stake was rancher independence and private property rights versus government encroachment.

- Hunters saw the bison as wildlife and believed they should have the opportunity to hunt them instead of having controlled shooting done by state game wardens or department of agriculture sharp-shooters. The values of the hunting groups were clear: wildlife should be managed using hunting as a tool, and they had the right to demand controlled sport hunting.

From this example, it's easy to see that there were major adaptive challenges centered on the emotional and deeply held beliefs, values, and habits of stakeholders. Failing to address these parts of the problem and just attempting a technical approach clearly would have been unwise.

So why is it that we often see those very kinds of solutions promoted? Leading groups of stakeholders to solve these kinds of adaptive problems requires hard work. It's also risky for the person(s) exercising the required leadership. The answer to the stakeholder groups working out their conflicts **does not exist** until the stakeholders work out a resolution they can all live with. Each stakeholder group that represents a set of beliefs and values has to decide what it is willing to "give up" in order to solve the problem. In other words, they have to **adapt** to be able to reach a solution. That's why these types of issues are called adaptive challenges.

Tools of Adaptive Leadership

A number of tools are needed to get groups of stakeholders with conflicting values and beliefs to resolve their adaptive issues. Usage of these tools is intertwined and best described as an "improvisational dance" (Marty Linsky, Harvard Kennedy School of Government, pers. comm.).

The books of Harvard professor, Ron Heifetz, et al. (2009, 2002, and 1994) provide a detailed treatment on addressing adaptive challenges. The rest of this chapter summarizes Heifetz's work and insights.

ADAPTIVE LEADERSHIP TOOL: FRAMING THE ADAPTIVE ISSUE

The person(s) performing the task of leading people to address an adaptive issue first must focus on framing. There are two kinds of framing: 1) framing the issue and 2) framing of the proposed action(s). Framing the issue is critical to creating a perspective through which the stakeholders can view the issue and begin to address it. Framing your intervention, or the proposed action(s) for getting the group to work toward solving the issue, applies to framing what actions may be taken for sound problem solving.

Framing the Issue

CASE EXAMPLE: THE IRON RANGER

Framing the issue is best done using the broadest context possible so that it can include the most options possible. An example of framing an issue occurred when one state agency asked me to help them with a meeting to decide how to develop a better "iron ranger." An iron ranger is a metal pipe set into concrete in the ground with a steel box welded onto it. The box has a slot in it through which campers and day users can deposit their camping and day-use fees. It's an easy way for an agency to collect money at a campsite or day-use area without having an employee onsite all the time. This particular problem arose when thieves broke into a number of iron rangers and stole the money.

The original question of "how to build a stronger iron ranger" was really an answer in disguise. The issue was actually broader than the iron ranger. The better question was: H*ow do we get the money from the campers' and day-use people's hands into the coffers of the agency*? The difference in this latter framing opened the avenues of solution to include many options in addition to a stronger iron ranger. For example, the best solution may have been using an online registration system where people pay with a credit card, or some other solution instead of just building a stronger steel box.

But how can you discern what the bigger, more important issue is for framing? A technique I recommend is asking "Why?" Do this a number of times until you get to what rings true as the real issue. In this case, when the group first stated that they needed to figure out how to build a better iron ranger, I asked: "Why do you need a better iron ranger?" When the answer was, "To prevent theft of the fees," I asked again, "Why do you need to prevent theft of fees?" The answer was something like, "Because we need the money from the campers and we are not getting it." So now the problem is framed as: *You are not getting the camping fees*, and the question can be framed as, "How can we remedy this?" This is a much broader framing than how to build a better iron ranger.

CASE EXAMPLE: WESTERN SOUTH DAKOTA OR STATEWIDE ISSUE

Another example of framing came from John Cooper, former director of South Dakota Game, Fish and Parks Department (pers. comm.). John needed to address the previously mentioned issue where landowners in western South Dakota wanted to be issued transferrable big-game permits that they could sell to hunters who would pay to hunt on their lands. This was a hugely popular idea in the western part of South Dakota, populated mostly by rural landowners. It's popularity in the western part of the state was enough to initially sway the governor at that time to support a bill that would authorize big-game license sales to landowners who could resell them. It was an adaptive issue where deeply held values and beliefs were involved. Landowner rights versus the North American model of wildlife management and public ownership of wildlife were the values at stake.

John realized that framing the issue solely as a western South Dakota matter was incorrect, especially when the majority of the state's population (and its sportsmen) lived in the urban areas in the eastern part of the state. John went to the governor and framed the issue as a **statewide** issue to which those in the eastern part of the state were greatly opposed. By framing the issue as a statewide issue, John was able to stop implementation of a narrow solution that favored a relatively small portion of state residents. This narrow solution would have created great discomfort for the governor from voters in the rest of the state. John Cooper stands by his statement that "Being able to determine the 'size of the boxing ring' is also critical when framing an issue." The boxing ring size in this case was the whole state, not just one part of it.

Will Harmon (pers. comm.), communications director with the Montana Consensus Council, further addressed framing or reframing of issues when he said:

> Another key to reframing an issue is to seek out the common ground among divided stakeholders and use that to frame the issue not as "us vs. them" but as a problem they all hold in common and that they all have a shared stake in resolving. I heard this "aha" moment from a stakeholder in a recreation use dispute: "You really can't solve a problem until you realize that your opponent on the other side of the table is also—has to be—your ally in finding a solution." Of course, stakeholders generally aren't inclined to see things from

their opponents' perspective, so I would serve as a neutral facilitator and interview the stakeholders and write up a report that summarized the areas of conflict and areas of agreement (the common ground) in a way that focused everyone on the shared nature of the problem. In this way, all the stakeholders saw that their voices contributed to framing the issue, and that their values and positions were being given due consideration. This one step made it much easier to bring divergent interests together in a constructive atmosphere and move the conversation forward.

Framing Your Intervention

Also, take advantage of the opportunity to frame your intervention into the adaptive issue. Framing your intervention into a problem environment where there are numerous stakeholders with conflicting values and beliefs may be done in two principle ways: 1) stating that you have "the answer" or, 2) framing the intervention as "this is an experiment for the group to try." Heifetz, et al. (2009) recommends that deciding which framing approach you choose should be based on the level of conflict among the stakeholders. If the conflict is low and stress levels are low, then people are more tolerant of trying experiments to see what works in solving the issue. However, if the conflict level is great and stress is high, then framing the intervention as "the answer" is often better because groups in or near crisis want answers and not experiments from their authority figures.

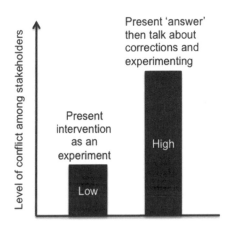

Remember, however, that adaptive problems do not have an answer until the stakeholders work one out amongst themselves. Don't fixate on the role of the knight on the white horse who comes in to save the day holding the right answer. You may believe in your answer, but it is the stakeholders that must do the adaptive work to develop their own answer with which they all can live.

In only one instance is it justifiable for the leadership role to present the answer. This is where the stress and conflict in the situation are so great that stakeholders are unable to work toward a solution and they revert to demanding the person leading the issue provide the answer. In this case, if you frame your intervention as *you have the answer*, then as soon as the stress in the system subsides to a lower level, begin talking about mid-course corrections and experimenting to find the best solution.

Creating a Holding Environment

In addition to framing the issue, a "holding environment" must be developed or selected. Heifetz et al. (2002) describes a holding environment this way:

> It may be a protected physical space you create by hiring an outside facilitator and taking a work group off-site to work through a particularly volatile and sensitive conflict. It may be the shared language and common history of a community that binds people together through trying times. . . . It may be characterized by a clear set of rules and processes that give minority voices the confidence that they will be heard without having to disrupt the proceedings to gain attention. A holding environment is a place where there is enough cohesion to offset the centrifugal forces that arises when people do adaptive work. In a holding environment, with structural, procedural, or virtual boundaries, people feel safe enough to address problems that are difficult, not only because they strain ingenuity, but also because they strain relationships.

Martin Luther King, Jr. used the church as a holding environment for the civil rights movement. A holding environment has structural, procedural, and/or virtual boundaries that may be defined as a space. A church can be literally a physical space, but it also has a history, set of beliefs, and a set of behaviors.

I used a governor's council to provide an environment for representation of different groups within a safe environment (Guynn 1997) to address Montana's private land access issues. It has been my experience that most state fish and wildlife agencies use some type of blue-ribbon panel, citizen's representation group, or committee as a holding environment for major adaptive issues. These groups may not be as fast or *efficient* in arriving at proposed solutions as one individual or a small like-minded group, but they are absolutely necessary for the real adaptive work that must be done by all stakeholders in order for them to arrive at an *effective* and successful solution.

Ripening the Issue

Ripeness refers to how much the issue is in the forefront of people's minds. Many of us have had the experience of going to an evening public meeting where we expected 25 or 30 participants and arrive to find 200! You know then that the issue the meeting was to address is a hot one with high public interest and concerns. Of course, we have had the opposite experience too. We arrive at a public meeting to find only one or two stakeholders attending. In this case, the issue needs ripening. In other words, the concern or interest in the collective stakeholders' minds needs to be increased.

There is a range within the spectrum of concern and interest that is most productive for groups of stakeholders to conduct the adaptive work needed. If the concerns and stress are too great and emotions too high, then the issue boils over and we may experience disruptive behaviors and the group is unable to do adaptive work. Conversely, if the stress is too low, then people are unwilling to expend the effort to address the problem and to suffer through the hard decisions about how much they are willing to give up in order to reach a solution.

My friend, Marty Linsky, with Harvard's Kennedy School of Government (pers. comm.), likens the ripening concept to using a pressure cooker to cook a vegetable stew. If the pressure is too low, then the vegetables don't cook and your stew is just crunchy vegetables. If the pressure in the cooker is too high, then it blows up and splatters your stew all over the kitchen. This leads to the next role of the person leading an adaptive challenge—regulating the pressure, better known as orchestrating the conflict.

Orchestrating the Conflict

Sometimes you may want to address an issue and the stakeholders do not have enough concern or interest to actively work on it. John Gardner

(1990) summed up this situation well as, "Apathy is rampant, but who cares!" In this situation, raising the pressure on the issue is a critical early step to success. John Kotter (1996) calls this creating a sense of urgency and says it is of overriding importance when leading change. The role of the person(s) leading the adaptive issue is to ensure that there is a sufficient level of urgency. Webster's Dictionary (1994) defines urgency as "of pressing importance." Don't confuse it with creating panic and unfounded concerns that inhibit people's ability to function rationally.

Creating a sense of urgency can be accomplished by any number of means. Choosing the means depends on the specific issue. Typically, making a proposal or taking an action is the easiest way for an agency to raise the pressure on an adaptive issue. But raising the level of concern is the antithesis to what most authority figures are expected to do. Remember that in the unspoken agreement, authority figures are expected to provide three things: **protection, order,** and **direction.** By raising the stress levels of stakeholders, you will be doing the opposite of what is expected of you by your stakeholders and your boss. This can be hazardous and career threatening because bosses (authority figures) are under pressure to maintain the low-stress environment of order and direction.

The Pressure Gauge for Adaptive Work

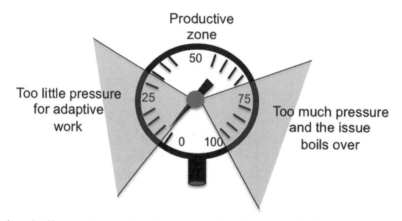

The challenge is to raise the stress level within the limits of what the stakeholders and your boss can stand, yet make it high enough to get action on the issue. No matter how strongly you feel about the adaptive issue, you do neither yourself nor anyone else any good by pushing too hard and creating such disequilibrium that you are de-authorized and become a martyr.

There is no ten-step program or specific process that can be called upon. It becomes an improvisational dance based on your skill and experience with the stakeholders, your own boss, and the agency. It is a matter of correctly reading others, empathizing with them, and understanding yourself and your natural reactions in order to choose the right level of intervention. This is often referred to as emotional intelligence and is addressed later in this chapter.

Many times an adaptive issue arises through no actions of your own. An issue boils over with ensuing conflicts and your agency is expected to "solve it." You get handed the hot potato and often you may try to provide the answer yourself. Remember this only works for technical problems.

When dealing with adaptive issues, solving it alone is really a form of maladaptive behavior for you and for your stakeholders. There's a great tendency for those in conflict to look to authority to solve problems for them. Those in authority often comply with pressure for a solution by trying to make a decision on the issue and to "be" the answer. Remember that **for adaptive issues, the stakeholders have to work out the solution based upon how much each stakeholder is willing to adapt to solve the problem.** Authority figures making an autocratic decision will not successfully solve an adaptive issue.

Often when handed a hot potato issue, the stress level among stakeholders is already high. The task is to lower the stress level below the boiling point so adaptive work can take place. Practices for lowering the concerns and stress in an adaptive situation can take many forms. Sometimes a cooling off period and slowing down the pace is useful, or addressing the technical parts of the issue first instead of the adaptive parts. For a more detailed listing of possible procedures, I suggest the book *The Practice of Adaptive Leadership* by Ron Heifetz, Alexander Grashow, and Marty Linsky (2009).

Giving the Work Back

One thing seems to me to be the most difficult for those leading an adaptive challenge. That is the difficulty the persons providing leadership have in letting go of the solution they personally want for the issue.

Your solution is not **their** solution. During seven years of conducting the National Conservation Leadership Institute (NCLI), the group of us who managed the NCLI asked each participant to bring a work-oriented issue to work on during their residency. One of the most common problems we encountered was NCLI fellows initially framing their issues as the difficulty of selling **their** personal solution to the other stakeholders.

When providing leadership to solve adaptive issues, you have to **give the work back** to the stakeholders involved. You can include sideboards of what your agency will not accept, but leave the solution development up to the stakeholders. Your agency can provide information and data if needed, but the adaptive problems reside in the contrasting deeply held values and beliefs of the stakeholders and not in a lack of logic or information. The sideboards your agency may wish to provide can be loosely categorized into three areas that bind the agency:

1. Legal Constraints (unless the stakeholders pursue legislation to provide for their agreed upon solution)
2. Financial Constraints (we can afford only so much, or don't come up with solutions that cost more money unless you come up with a way to raise the money).
3. Biological/Technical Constraints (what is the minimum viable population of animals acceptable, maximum sustained yield from a population, and other biological and technical parameters).

Decision Pyramid

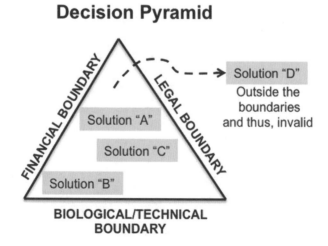

These sideboards can be envisioned as a pyramid that encompasses the agency's solution space. A group representing all stakeholders can derive solutions from anywhere within the triangle but not outside.

Within these sideboards, the work must be **given back** to the stakeholders for them to work out a solution. The stakeholders represent through their values and beliefs the socio-political boundaries within which the decision must be contained. It is important to remember that just because an option is within one of the boundaries (for example, the biological boundary) does not mean it is within all of the other boundaries.

It is important to realize that you **won't know** if the solution the stakeholders settle upon will look like A, B, or C. That should be okay as long as it's within the sideboards you set. You can be comfortable that a solution like D will not be developed because it is outside the boundaries for solutions. Giving back the work requires **letting go of your personal solution** and opening the door to an as-of-yet undefined solution, but one with sideboards.

Giving the work back seems simple enough. However, like all things in life, it's seldom as simple in practice as it appears in theory. Some of the difficulties include stakeholder reluctance to do the hard work of having to decide what they're willing to give up in order to reach a solution. Stakeholders will frequently turn to authority figures to solve the problem for them. In most cases this is your agency. Don't be sucked into this tempting dilemma. It is enticing to think you have the answer for the stakeholders, but only technical problems can be solved this way. If you choose to decide an adaptive issue as the authority figure, then either one group of stakeholders is satisfied and the others are angry with you, or you make a compromise. Like Solomon splitting the baby, all stakeholders then will be dissatisfied with your decision.

Recognizing Work Avoidance

Stakeholders' reluctance to take on the necessary adaptive work is what Heifetz and Linsky (2002) refer to as work avoidance. Some of the ways groups exhibit *work avoidance* are:

- Ignoring the issue
- Identifying whoever raises the issue as "the problem"

- Applying a technical fix
- Scapegoating
- Assigning to a powerless committee

There are many other creative ways groups devise to avoid doing the hard work of solving adaptive issues. The point is that if you are leading stakeholders to solve an adaptive issue, you must be diligent in watching for work avoidance. Bringing the group back on track to address the real adaptive issue is part of providing leadership.

Ensuring Equal Power

One of the other things to watch for when leading conflicting groups is power imbalances. Addressing adaptive issues works best when all the stakeholders are equally powerful—or equally powerless—in their amount of influence in shaping a solution.

CASE EXAMPLE: GAME FARMS IN THE MIDWEST

An example of what happened in a Midwestern state's Department of Natural Resources (DNR) a few years ago illustrates this point.

Background

I was requested to meet with a group of legislators, game farmers, sportsmen, and DNR staff. The issue was how to stop the spread of chronic wasting disease from outside the state into state deer herds while the state's game farmers wanted to continue to import and export deer. The DNR had already tried to pass a regulation banning game farmers from importing and exporting captive deer. In return, the game farmers threatened to pass legislation to transfer control of game farms from DNR to the state department of agriculture. (Interestingly, the game farmers had the votes in the state legislature to get this passed.) The DNR relented and asked me to help the group of game farmers, legislators, sportsmen, and DNR staff put together a process for the stakeholders to work out a solution. All agreed to try and work together to solve the problem.

I helped representatives from the legislature, DNR, and the interest groups put together a process to work on this adaptive issue. The deeply held values and beliefs in conflict were: private business rights and resistance to government (DNR) infringement on the one side, and on the other side were the values and beliefs regarding the safety of the state deer population and acceptable levels of risk in order to promote private business.

After the group designed a process for stakeholders to address the issue, several months of concentrated effort by all the stakeholders followed. But there was a critical flaw. No one foresaw that the game farmers had enough votes in the legislature to get their own solution approved without having to consider the needs or wants of other stakeholders. After months of trying to work out a solution, the game farmers were unwilling to make any concessions and finally withdrew from the process.

The learning point for me was to ensure in the future that all stakeholders were equally powerful or powerless when it came to getting their way with regard to the adaptive issue solution. In hindsight, I realized that I could have recommended to the DNR that they level the playing field by asking the governor to support the stakeholder process to work out a solution to the issue. The governor could have then told all stakeholders that he would veto any bill introduced by a stakeholder group as an end run around the process. This would have ensured all had to come to the table to work out a solution.

Involving the Stakeholders

Hans and Annemarie Bleiker are part of the Institute for Participatory Management and Planning (IPMP) in Monterey, California. They are well known as gurus in the field of citizen participation. The practices, principles, and techniques they teach are recommended as the basis for any stakeholder involvement effort (Bleiker 1986).

Here are several factors that I have found that are critical for success when involving stakeholders in a holding environment to address adaptive issues.

Factor One: Involve **all** potentially affected interests (this includes any stakeholders who are actually affected by the issue or even think they are affected). The surest way to fail is to leave out one or more stakeholder groups. This does not mean that all stakeholders as **individuals** must be part of the process. Some individuals are too disruptive or entrenched to allow the process to work. But representatives of all **interest groups** must be included. Remember, the best argument to stop an adaptive solution is not the merits of the solution, but the statement: *We were not included!*

Factor Two: Representatives of stakeholder groups must regularly go back to the constituents they represent and keep them updated with the discussions, tradeoffs, and decisions made in the holding environment (committee, council, panel, etc.). The representatives have the responsibility to explain decisions and tradeoffs made by the representatives of each stakeholder group and to get buy in from their stakeholder group. Otherwise you end up with the representatives in the holding environment agreeing while all the stakeholders throughout the state are still disagreeing.

This means the stakeholder representatives in the holding environment must do the hard adaptive work of giving up some things and then perform the leadership task of disappointing (at some level) their own constituents back home. After all, to solve the issue, some tradeoffs will be necessary. Each stakeholder representative must decide how much he or she can disappoint their constituents and still remain an authority figure to them.

Factor Three: Don't allow stakeholder representatives to send a substitute if they cannot attend a meeting in the holding environment. My experience has been that if substitutes are permitted, then individual representatives for interest groups may come to one meeting but send someone else to the next meeting. If each stakeholder group has different representatives each time the group convenes, it amounts to having a new group for each meeting. The group will have to go over old ground each meeting and reconfirm and reopen decisions made in past meetings. Progress grinds to a halt (Guynn 1997).

DANGER AND CAUTIONS

A caution for those of you courageous enough to take on leadership of adaptive challenges: don't do it alone. It's too easy to get isolated and disempowered if you tackle adaptive challenges alone. Enlist the help of allies in your adaptive work, but don't use allies as confidants.

Heifetz and Linsky (2002) distinguish allies from confidants. A *confidant* is someone you can confide in who is interested in you and your welfare but has no stake in the adaptive issue. An *ally* is someone with a stake in the issue who is willing to help you perform leadership tasks and give you their opinions. Do not confuse these two roles. The danger is that if you confide in one or more of your allies, then at some point in the process they may have conflicting loyalties regarding their constituents and loyalty to you. It's wiser not to put your allies or yourself in this position. Keep your confidants separate from allies.

As I've said before, taking a leadership role in helping stakeholder groups address adaptive issues is hazardous work. It involves your disappointing stakeholders by not making the decision for them (of course each group wants your decision to be in *their* favor). It means you have to take on the challenge of orchestrating conflict to keep the stakeholders at high enough stress levels to be in the productive zone and yet not blow up the process. This disappoints all stakeholders, your employees, and your boss who collectively expect you, as an authority figure, to restore calm and solve the problem.

Sometimes we have no choice and a hot issue is thrust upon us. At these times, it's best to understand the difference between adaptive and technical issues and what will be required in solving adaptive issues. You can then design a process that has the best chance of working. John Cooper, former Director of South Dakota Game, Fish and Parks (pers. comm.), says that your legislators and governor will "love you" for using an adaptive process because it allows them to avoid taking sides on the issue. The political officials can point to the adaptive, public process being implemented and refuse to take action personally until the process has had a chance to be completed. This allows the politicians to avoid taking sides and potentially disenfranchising segments of voters.

Adaptive work, as defined in this chapter, is the lens through which I believe leadership is best viewed for state fish and wildlife agencies! Technical work as defined in this chapter may be challenging but is fairly simple to apply because technical answers are available. Simply providing technical answers is not really leadership, but it can be considered as a use of authority to provide the technical answers and help people organize to implement those answers. Again, this is just good administrative work. As Heifetz (1994) says, "Adaptive work, however, consists of helping groups gain the learning required to address conflicts in the values people hold, or to diminish the gap between the values people stand for an the reality they face."

Helping groups address conflicts in values is *people work*. It requires a myriad of skills and understanding of human behavior, attitudes, and styles. How well you can work with and interpret the actions and feelings of others is paramount to making good decisions about when and what type of intervention to try in any given situation. This is the ability to do the *improvisational dance* of effectively leading others to develop adaptive solutions.

Social Cognition and Emotional Intelligence

The characterization of leadership activities as an *improvisational dance* captures the fact that there are no set steps to follow and the person providing leadership has to adjust their actions to the situation and stakeholders' mindset in real time. It is a matter of observing the stakeholder groups, attempting to intervene, and watching to see if it works to bring the stakeholders closer to addressing or solving the issue. Based upon the reaction of the stakeholders, the person in the leadership role then designs another intervention to move the process forward. This skill of understanding individuals and groups and how they will react to your interventions involves *social cognition and emotional intelligence.*

The greater your social cognition skills, the more likely your leadership activities are to succeed. Fisk and Taylor (1991) define social cognition as "How people make sense of other people and themselves." Their work addresses factors such as attribution theory or how the perceiver uses information to arrive at causal explanations for events. They discuss social schema as expectations and effects—in other words, the fact that **we all make assumptions about other people, the situations, and ourselves.**

These factors explain our interactions with others and play a critical role in how we attempt to make leadership interventions. Some people seem to have a knack for doing this better than others. I believe that this is one of the main reasons that we tend to describe some people as "natural leaders." It is a layperson's way of explaining why some people seem innately more successful working with and leading others.

Daniel Goleman (1998) characterizes a combination of the social cognition characteristics as *emotional intelligence.* His work tends to connect social cognition to actions in the work place and its effects on one's

success or failure. Goleman defines the framework for emotional competence as having two main categories with subsets for each:

Personal Competence
- Self –Awareness
- Self-Regulation
- Motivation

Social Competence
- Empathy for others
- Social Skills

LEARNING EMOTIONAL INTELLIGENCE

The better we are at these above skills, the easier it is to make successful
leadership interventions in adaptive work. In other words, to choose the
right steps in the *improvisational dance*. Know when to "sit this one out,"
when to "use a quick step," or when the "music of the situation requires
a slow step."

These skills can be learned, but not as one might expect. Most of us
are used to learning knowledge through studying while in the educational
system. That is cognitive knowledge—learned facts that we can apply.
However, this alone will not increase our emotional intelligence. Just
knowing we should not behave angrily in a specific situation does not
keep us from doing so. Just as knowing we should not smoke and all the
health risks associated with it does not necessarily keep us from smoking.

Learning to improve our emotional intelligence requires something
different than simple cognitive learning of facts. We must learn social
cognition skills through **forcing** ourselves to do something we know will
be more effective in a specific situation instead of using our emotional
default reaction. It requires forcing ourselves to select a different behavior than our default behavior for a situation. This takes **discipline** and
effort. The good news is that every time we force ourselves to use a different behavior for that situation, it becomes easier.

Our neural pathways are strengthened for a new behavior as we continue to repeatedly apply the new behavior over time. Correspondingly
the old, default behavior pathways atrophy over time. Thus, improving
our emotional intelligence requires experiencing situations repeatedly over time and using discipline to select new, better behaviors.

Like learning to play music, or to dance, it takes repeated experience through practice.

IT'S ABOUT PEOPLE, TRUST, AND RELATIONSHIPS

Emotional intelligence is important for successfully conducting many leadership activities. This is because a significant number of leadership activities are directed at influencing others. Trust is a basic building block for influencing others, creating followership, and leading.

Many times when conducting agency reviews, I have observed that if trust levels are low within the agency, then nothing works—nothing in terms of employees working together to achieve agency results and nothing in terms of "fixes" to improve the agency situation. The first thing that must be done is to build back a basic level of trust before any organizational fixes can be implemented and organizational results improved.

Stephen Covey (1991) makes the case that trust with others is based upon personal trustworthiness. Our daily, personal actions influence others' opinions of us and our trustworthiness with them. If follows then, that our daily personal actions impact our ability to influence and lead others. Building trust begins with modeling the behaviors we desire in others. It cannot be a matter of *do as I say and not as I do.*

Next is relating to others—using emotional intelligence to understand others, and empathy to relate to them appropriately. Books have been written about these personal behaviors as related to leadership (Stephen M. R. Covey 2006, and Stephen R. Covey 2004, 1991). I will not attempt to cover this broad topic other than to emphasize that leadership is closely tied to working with others, and your ability to do so is influenced greatly by your ability to engender trust through behaving in trustworthy ways.

The concepts of trust and trustworthiness boil down to values. How do your personal values compare with what is regarded as high or good values of others and society in general? Consistently behaving in ways that exhibit your shared values with groups you wish to influence is critical to the ability to gain trust and perform effective leadership activities.

Summary

The definition of leadership I find most useful in working with state fish and wildlife agencies is: leading people to deal with adaptive issues and to bring about change to meet socially useful goals while attaining a higher moral level. In summary, we can think of leadership in this context as a series of important points:

- Leadership is an activity or an exercise—not a person.
- Leadership is not done by anyone all the time.
- Since leadership is an activity, it can be learned.
- Exercising leadership is different from exercising authority.
- Maintaining authority means fulfilling the unspoken contract between the authority figure, their boss, and subordinates in that the authority figure provides protection, order, and direction.
- Successful leadership results in bringing about significant change.
- Leadership is hazardous because people fear loss associated with change.
- Exercising leadership requires your making others uncomfortable, but at a level that they can stand.
- Leadership is about taking "smart risks" for a purpose and not becoming a martyr.
- Risk taking leadership actions only for purposes in which you strongly believe.

Sometimes you may see an adaptive issue that everyone is avoiding, and you may decide to induce the stakeholders to address it. The only reason to take on such hazardous work is because of your own sense of purpose. What's important to you? Is it important enough to take the risks associated with leading others to address the challenge? Max Peterson, chief emeritus of the U.S. Forest Service (pers. comm.), once said to me, "Your legacy is the result of how you handle a half dozen 'significant events' in your whole career!" Usually those significant events are adaptive in nature.

Performing leadership activities successfully requires the ability to influence others. This is emotional work and requires people skills described best as emotional intelligence. Without emotional intelligence, your ability to successfully interact with others and perform leadership activities will be greatly hindered.

Trust is a critical product of your successful interactions with others. Trust is the basis from which interventions can be launched to achieve successful adaptive leadership activities. This trust is based upon others' perception of your trustworthiness. This, in turn, is based upon you consistent modeling of values that others find congruent with their own sets of values. Given this, your everyday actions constantly either encourage trust or discourage it. Thus "leadership is a full time job because your daily actions determine your trustworthiness to lead" (Corky Pugh, pers. comm.).

Trust and trustworthiness are value-laden attributes that generate emotions. Leadership is about managing your own emotions as well as other's. The next chapter deals with the brain functions in relation to emotions, how a science mantra of impartiality in the fish and wildlife profession is critical but can be overused especially when communicating with our publics.

Literature Cited

Animal Plant and Health Inspection Service. 2012. http://www.aphis.usda. gov/animal_health/animal_dis_spec/cattle/downloads/cattle-bison. pdf. 5 pp.

Bass, Bernard. 2008. *Bass and Stodgdill's Handbook on Leadership: Theory, Research and Managerial Applications* (4th. ed.). The Free Press, New York, NY. 623 pp.

Blanchard, Ken. 2010. *Leading from a Higher Level*. BMC publishing as FT Press. Upper Saddle River, NJ. 362 pp.

Bleiker H. and Annemarie Bleiker. 1986. *Citizen Participation Handbook*. Fifth Ed. Institute for Participative Mgmt. Monterey, CA.

Burns, James McGregor. 1978. *Leadership*. Harper Colophon. New York, NY. 530 pp.

Carlyle, Thomas. 1841. *On Heroes, Hero-Worship, and the Heroic in History*. James Fraser Publishers. London. 393 pp.

Covey, Stephen R. 1991. *Principle-Centered Leadership*. Simon & Schuster. New York, NY. 334 pp.

_____2004. *The 7 Habits of Highly Effective People*. Free Press, Simon & Schuster. New York, NY. 372 pp.

_____2004. *The 8th Habit: From Effectiveness to Greatness*. Free Press, Simon & Schuster. New York, NY. 409 pp.

Covey, Stephen M. R. *The Speed of Trust: The One Thing that Changes Everything*. Free Press, Simon & Schuster. New York, NY. 384 pp.

Dickson, Tom. 2014. "Where are All the Elk?" *Montana Outdoors*. Sept-Oct. Montana Fish, Wildlife & Parks. Helena, MT. pp. 34-39.

Fisk, Susan T. and Shelly E. Taylor. 1991. *Social Cognition*. McGraw-Hill, Inc. New York, NY. 718 pp.

Gardner, J. W. 1990. *John W. Gardner on Leadership*. The Free Press, Simon and Schuster. New York, NY. 220 pp.

Goleman, Daniel. 2006. *Working with Emotional Intelligence*. Bantam Dell. New York, NY. 383 pp.

Guynn, Dwight. 1999. "Leadership Development in the Fish and Wildlife Profession." Transcript, North American Wildlife and Natural Resources Conference. (64). pp. 538-548.

_____1997. "Miracle in Montana—Managing Conflicts over Private Lands and Pubic Wildlife Issues." Transcript, North American Wildlife and Natural Resources Conference. (62). pp. 146-154.

_____1997. "A Case Study of Citizen Participation as a Success Model for Natural Resource Problems." *Wildlife Society Bulletin*. (25). pp. 392-398.

_____1979. Management of Deer Hunters on Private Land in Colorado. Ph.D. Diss. Colo. St. Univ. Fort Collins, CO. 253 pp.

Heifetz, R. and M. Linsky. 2002. *Leadership on the Line*. Harvard Business School Press. Boston, MA. 252 pp.

Heifetz R., A. Grashow, M. Linsky. 2009. *The Practice of Adaptive Leadership*. Harvard Business Press. Boston, MA. 326 pp.

Heifetz, Ron. 1999. *Leadership without Easy Answers*. Belknap Press of Harvard Univ. Cambridge, MA. 348 pp.

Hersey, Paul. *The Situational Leader*. 1985. Center for Leadership Studies. Centerville, MA. 128 pp.

Kotter, John. 2008. *A Sense of Urgency*. Harvard Business Press. Boston, MA. 196 pp.

_____1996. *Leading Change*. Harvard Business School Press. Boston, MA. 187 pp.

Lehr, Honah. 2010. *How We Decide*. First Mariner Books. New York, NY. pp. 13-16. 302 pp.

Machiavelli, Niccolo. 1992. *The Prince*. Dover Publications. New York, NY. 71 pp.

Pac, H. I., and K. Frey. 1991. "Some Population Characteristics of the Northern Yellowstone Bison Herd during the Winter of 1988-89." Montana Department of Fish, Wildlife & Parks, Bozeman, MT. 29 pp.

Prukop, Joanna and R. Regan. 2005. "The Value of the North American Model of Wildlife Conservation—an International Association of Fish and Wildlife Agencies position." *Wildlife Society Bulletin.* 33(1) pp. 374-377.

Rounds, R. C. 1975. *Public Access to Private Lands for Hunting.* Colorado Division of Wildlife. Report No. 2. 179 pp.

Webster's Dictionary. 1994. *Webster's II New Riverside University Dictionary.* The Riverside Publishing Co., Houghton Mifflin, Co. Boston, MA.

CHAPTER SIX

Emotion, Science, and Communication

The profession of fish and wildlife management is a scientific field where professionals must be objective, detached, and impartial. This is crucial when conducting animal research and when practicing wildlife population management. Work in the wildlife field requires focusing on the welfare of entire populations of animals instead of on individual animals. For example, it may require the harvest (killing) of a portion of a wildlife population annually to keep that population in balance with its available food sources.

But wildlife management is also set in a context of constituents' strongly held emotions and values. Scientists are supposed to remain above this emotional quagmire and provide unbiased and objective data. Sometimes scientists fail to remain unbiased and are castigated for their lapse. Noted wildlife scientist Valerius Geist (2013) suggests that some scientists fail to remain impartial in conducting scientific research, stating, "There is no shortage of advocacy masquerading as science, as well as lamentable flaws inflicted by scientists themselves, from outright fraud to laziness and inexcusable thoughtlessness." The point is that the practice of wildlife science and the determination of scientific research facts need to be performed with complete objectivity. Yet it is important to recognize a major distinction between sciences: *wildlife science* and the *science of communicating* wildlife facts are **two different things.**

Communications: The Science versus the Emotion

State agency wildlife professionals are state government employees. As such, they are frequently discouraged from advocacy concerning public wildlife issues. Objectivity is stressed, partly to prevent a publicly funded agency from promoting the views of specific interest groups. The impartiality of a scientific approach and the discouragement of public agencies promoting specific interest group's views both emphasize the objectivity of wildlife science. These practices also ignore the use of emotion in communication of that science.

The concept of presenting data objectively is based upon the incorrect assumption that facts and logic are all that is needed to influence the public in its decisions. Communication science, however, recommends delivering your message with some passion, letting people see who you are and what you stand for.

Where in the Brain Decisions Are Made

The science of communication relies on an understanding of human decision processes. It involves comprehending how the brain actually functions in decision-making and the critical role of emotions. Our complex brain governs all our actions, including our thoughts, emotions, and decisions. For the purpose of this chapter, I will define emotion as a thought process based on the sequence of observation, interpretation (including assumptions), and the resulting behavioral responses.

Observation → **Interpretation** → **Response**

Emotional responses are based on a combination of chemical reactions in the brain that produce what we call feelings. These chemical reactions and resultant feelings are the foundational mix from where we choose our responses, often rapidly in reflex mode.

When we communicate with our publics, we want to influence their brains to create those specific emotions that will facilitate the behavioral responses we desire from them. For example, the desired responses might be donating money for wildlife or voting on a wildlife issue.

Dr. Tom Kalouse (pers. comm.), a clinical psychologist in Denver, Colorado, made this profound statement: "People make decisions based upon their emotions and then use logic and facts to justify their decisions!" Could this be true? When I first heard this, I refused to believe that I made decisions emotionally. As a certified wildlife biologist, I'd always considered my decision-making to be logical and scientifically based. However, once Tom explained the biology of various brain functions, I came to understand the fallacy of my previous belief.

Tom described the prefrontal lobes of the brain as the "executive center" where facts are considered and logic is applied. But he also explained that decisions are not made in the brain's executive center. Where decisions are actually made is in the brain's "decision center," or its limbic system that includes the thalamus, hypothalamus, amygdala, hippocampus, and basal ganglia.

The limbic system is the area of the brain that regulates emotion and memory. **People make decisions in this emotional center of the brain!** This part of the brain is not associated with our language skills and, consequently, has no language. This is why we often say things like, "I *feel* this is the right decision."

Tom even described a case where a male patient's limbic system was damaged during a surgery. Thereafter, the patient was never able to make a decision. The patient could list all the alternatives for a decision and the pros and cons of each, but he was incapable of deciding. Consequently, the patient lost his job and was permanently impaired from living a normal life, all due to limbic system damage.

Since decisions are made in the portion of the brain that is the emotional center, doesn't it follow that to influence people's decisions it would be important to address this part of the brain? In other words, **it is unwise to ignore people's emotions when trying to influence their decisions.** Yet this is exactly what wildlife agencies regularly do when relaying solely on uninspiring data in a completely objective fashion. Attempting to influence people's decisions by relying on facts and logic alone is like trying to convince people to buy sushi by describing it as "cold, dead fish." Even adding more data like the scientific name of the species of fish, its temperature, or the date of its demise does not work! Emotions are what drive human decisions.

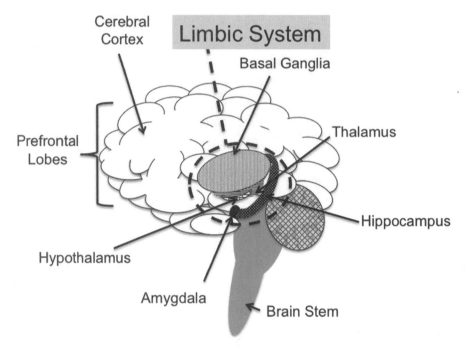

Human Brain

Consider how other organizations and businesses use the concept of emotion-laden communication so successfully. You have probably seen advertisements seeking donations for various causes. The Society for Prevention of Cruelty to Animals (SPCA), United Nations International Children's Emergency Fund (UNICEF), and the Wounded Warrior Project are examples of organizations that successfully use emotion to elicit desired responses from their audiences—usually the act of donating money.

Notice that these organizations' television advertisements don't use a "talking head" on your television screen spewing numerous facts about how many animals or children are served, nor the statistics of needs, etc. Instead, as a viewer you see footage of emaciated dogs and cats with ribs showing and sad eyes seeming to plead for help. Up-close images of poor, starving children with pleading eyes or of wounded veterans with missing limbs or burn scars are images calculated to elicit a strong emotional response. The emotion prompted by portrayal of these images is very effective in gaining the desired viewer decisions to donate funds. These organizations have learned that logic and facts alone are not sufficient!

Crossing Implicit Lines

If an agency was to use emotion in its presentation of data, then how could it be done without crossing the undefined lines of advocacy? For example, state wildlife agencies often testify in legislative proceedings either favorably or unfavorably toward proposed legislation. While an anti-hunting group may testify using emotionally slanted graphics depicting the shooting of wild animals and emotionally charged language, the wildlife agency typically refrains from such activities. Is it correct, for example, to show starving fawn photos or graphic pictures of starvation within under-harvested wildlife populations when the agency presents a case for hunting? To date, most wildlife agencies have used mostly data and facts when communicating. Some agencies have no choice in this decision because they are part of a larger department such as a department of natural resources that will not allow use of emotions in communicating with publics. In such instances, I urge those agencies to work with their larger department to convince them of the importance of showing emotion.

I believe this is why anti-hunting and anti-trapping groups gain support in spite of the facts and logic that hunting and trapping are valuable wildlife management tools. These "anti"-groups effectively use emotion instead of facts to sway members of the public. I believe that if wildlife professionals are going to effectively influence their publics, then they need to take advice from communication experts and use not only logic and facts, but address the emotional aspects of issues as well.

One state wildlife agency uses the acronym POMT to analyze its audience for communication efforts. The letters represent the process of defining the:

Problem to be addressed
Objective of the information effort
Message to be delivered
Technique used to deliver the message

Once audience analysis is completed using the POMT approach then, the actual communication approach can be denoted by the acronym

RACES. Judy Stokes (pers. comm.), a retired communication professional who worked for New Hampshire Fish and Game Department, uses the acronym RACES as follows:

Research

Action Planning (audience messages, strategies, and tactics)

Communication

Evaluation

Stewardship (of the change in what people feel, know, and do)

How often have your agency's wildlife professionals or even director's office staff effectively used or been able to use emotion in communications with your publics or media? Do they use anything like POMT or RACES techniques to gain greater understanding of the audience in order to ascertain how best to reach them? If permission is needed from a larger department to use emotion in communications, then work on getting it. If staff does not understand the concepts of POMT or RACES, then training is in order. Most of all, do not let the scientific concept of impartiality cloud the need for appropriately using emotion to communicate scientific information.

What about presenting the agency's different programs or proposals for funding to constituents? Is this an appropriate time to use emotion? How might this be done? Simon Sinek based his popular book, *Start with Why* (Sinek 2009), upon the simple understanding of relationships between the biology of the brain and human decision-making. Sinek's basic premise, like that of Tom Kalouse, is that for organizations to succeed with their constituents, these organizations need to reach out to people's emotions through first explaining their organization's purpose (their "why"). It seems critically important that state fish and wildlife agencies give people something to emotionally connect with before addressing the facts of what the agency does or how it goes about it. Sinek illustrates this concept quite well with his statement, "Martin Luther King, Jr. gave an I *Have a Dream* speech, not an I *Have a Plan* speech" (Sinek, 2009).

But using emotion-generating techniques when communicating doesn't mean that data and facts can be totally ignored. It means that to rely solely on logic will be much less successful than a two-pronged approach using emotional appeal as well as logic.

Becoming an advocate on a particular subject is not always appropriate for a wildlife agency. For example, advocating a position on a subject that will not biologically affect wildlife, such as how a specific number of nonresident licenses will be distributed, may not fall within the agency's boundaries for using emotion. What I see, however, is that wildlife agencies often testify against legislation that contradicts good wildlife biology. Wildlife agencies also propose and support wildlife regulations when communicating with their commissions and publics as part of the regulation-setting process. At minimum, these are instances where agency staff needs to use emotions as part of the message presented by the agency. In other words, choose when to advocate using emotion.

A POSSIBLE CASE SCENARIO
Here is an example of deciding when it is appropriate to combine emotion with the presentation of information and facts. An anti-trapping group is promoting the banning of all trapping on public lands. The anti-trapping group's public campaign used emotion-evoking pictures and stories of pet dogs caught in traps. If the wildlife agency were firmly opposed to losing trapping as a management tool, would you consider it appropriate for the wildlife agency to show a young boy tearful over loss of his 4-H lamb to wolves that may no longer be trapped on any public lands if the legislation is passed?

The facts: a wolf killed the lamb and wolf predation would be less controlled if trapping were eliminated on all public lands. Does the agency just state these bland facts with a "talking head," or does it show pictures or video of the boy with the lamb carcass as an appeal to people's emotions? The same information is being presented. It is a matter of whether information is presented within an emotional context or solely as facts. In addition, the presentation may be different for each audience. For example, legislators may be more affected by financial considerations, policy matters, or facts related to public opinions than the average citizen.

AN AGENCY CASE EXAMPLE: DISASTER FROM
TOO MUCH OBJECTIVITY AND TOO LITTLE EMOTION
Sometimes, in spite of the best intentions, agencies make major public blunders when taking logical actions that blindly follow the scientific

mantra of *no emotional attachments*. While the following example related to me happened in the 1980s, the lessons learned still apply today.

A fish and wildlife agency operated a fish hatchery in a remote part of the state. The hatchery was a favorite place for local school classes to visit. A grade school class donated several ring-necked pheasants to the hatchery as part of a class project. The hatchery manager had some small pens built, and the pheasants and their progeny lived there for a number of years.

As pheasants in captivity are prone to do, they increased their numbers over time. This increased the costs and time for hatchery staff to feed and care for the birds. Over the years, what began, as a small project totally outside of the hatchery's mission became an increasing burden for all of the hatchery staff. When the fish hatchery got a new manager, the manager recognized the problem and made a decision to get rid of the birds.

As you read this you probably can recognize the potential for a media disaster in the making. But put yourself in the shoes of the hatchery manager. He has newly accepted responsibility for overall management of the fish hatchery. The birds are a side project that has nothing to do with the mission of the hatchery, and the pheasants are draining resources, manpower, and finances that are needed for the production of fish. The hatchery manager is making the right *logical* decision.

The hatchery employed several high school boys in the evening and on the weekends to help with work around the hatchery. The hatchery manager told these boys that it was their job to get rid of the pheasants. Then he gave each boy a baseball bat and sent them into the pheasant pen. You can imagine the carnage that ensued as a bunch of teenagers began swinging bats at pheasants fluttering and flying within the confines of the pen.

When the teenage boys arrived back in their school classes the next day, they did not remain silent about the event. *Guess what we did yesterday*? Before long, word was out in the whole community. The local press got involved, and it was a media disaster for the hatchery and the agency. The grade school felt betrayed. The community believed that the agency, and specifically the hatchery staff, were heartless and should not be in charge of the state's natural resources. In hindsight, this public relations disaster was easily avoidable, but it required forethought about public perception and emotions.

The first learning point from this event is that even though an agency may be making the right logical decision based on hard, cold, facts, how that decision is implemented needs to be considered in light of public scrutiny. Setting the pheasants free may have been a better decision even though the biological reality is that survival of released pheasants would have been minimal at best. Secondly, no matter how remote the location or how few people are involved, the actions taken must be acceptable to the public at large. Word will assuredly leak out!

AN AGENCY CASE EXAMPLE WHERE EMOTION WORKED

Max Petersen, chief emeritus of the U.S. Forest Service, relayed a story to me about how impactful an agency's showing of emotion can be. Max's story dealt with an outbreak of disease at a research facility studying ducks near Washington, D.C. The disease infesting the facilities' research ducks was very contagious; therefore, all the ducks at the research facility would need to be euthanized to ensure that the disease did not spread to populations of wild ducks.

The press had become aware that the research facility, which was supposed to be working to help ducks, was going to euthanize all the ducks at the facility. This sounded like a good piece for the evening news, and a reporter and camera team were sent to interview the top folks at the facility.

The facility director and some of the top scientists met with the reporter and cameraman and spoke at length about the facts of the disease including its life history, how it was spread, and why the ducks had to be euthanized. This "talking head" session was all dutifully recorded on tape. Then, as the reporters were leaving the facility and crossing the parking lot, a research technician stepped out of the building's side door for a smoke break. Always alert for news opportunities, the reporter and cameraman walked over and did an impromptu interview with the technician.

The technician related how he had helped care for the ducks at the facility and that the ducks were really special to him. He spoke with a catch in his voice about how heartbreaking it was to have to euthanize these animals. At just this moment, a wild duck flew above the treetops and the technician pointed to it and said that while it was heartbreaking to have to euthanize the research facility ducks, it was necessary in order to protect all the wild ducks that were out there.

You can guess which footage made the evening news. The point is that we need not rely on happenstance to get it right with the media. We need to be smart about using and showing our own emotions appropriately. Appearing to be the heartless scientist with little to no feeling does not play well with our publics.

AN AGENCY CASE EXAMPLE WHERE ONE SIDE
USES EMOTION AND THE OTHER DOESN'T

An example previously mentioned regarding bison also illustrates how the use of emotion, or lack thereof, can influence public perception. To recap: Yellowstone National Park (the park) sustained major forest fire damage during the early fall of 1988. The winter that followed was one of the worst winters Montana had experienced in recent history. Both of these events combined to have a major impact on the bison herds in the park by reducing their available food sources. It was generally recognized that bison numbers in the park were greatly above the carrying capacity of the winter range food sources. When the snow piled up and food became scarce, the bison began to migrate to lower elevations outside the park onto private lands in search of food.

The problem was exacerbated because, at that time, anywhere from one third to one half of the bison in the park tested positive for a disease called brucellosis. Most states, including Montana, had been successful in eradicating brucellosis from their domestic livestock herds and achieving a statewide brucellosis-free rating. If any state is not certified brucellosis free, then additional costs and efforts are required to test all cattle destined to be shipped outside that state's boundaries.

Montana's brucellosis-free certification was perceived to be jeopardized when infected bison began to migrate out of Yellowstone Park in record numbers that winter. As bison numbers swelled outside the park, the agricultural community was adamant that something be done to keep the bison from potentially infecting livestock on nearby ranches. If even one cattle herd contracted brucellosis, then the state was in danger of losing its brucellosis-free status. Thus, stockgrowers in Montana, including those who did not even reside near Yellowstone Park, were very concerned.

Since bison were considered wildlife, the problem came to rest squarely on the shoulders of FWP. Previously, the director had made a plea to the legislature to allow FWP game wardens to try to drive bison back into the park and to shoot bison that remained outside the park. Several sportsmen's groups were against game wardens shooting bison and felt that sportsmen should be allowed to perform this task through controlled hunts. Since hunting is prohibited inside Yellowstone Park, all taking of bison would need to occur on other state, federal, or private lands adjacent to the park.

The legislature, against the wishes of FWP, decided to allow hunters to kill the bison that could not be driven back into the park. FWP realized that this was a real publicity disaster in the making because non-hunting publics would be emotionally inflamed by "sport hunting" of public bison from a national park. But FWP's hands were tied and the agency was going to have to make the best of a bad situation. Emotion was going to be a major part of the process in dealing with this issue.

Hunters were drawn for bison harvest tags and they began a systematic elimination of bison outside the park. As expected, anti-hunting groups descended on the areas where hunts were occurring and the press had a field day.

Footage was seen on national television almost nightly about the killing of America's bison in Montana. Scenes were shown of bison standing placidly in several feet of snow as a hunter moved close to the unalarmed, park-like animal for a shot. Then we saw the hunter shoot the bison and blood covering the snow as the animal drops and kicks its last. Talk about emotional television footage for the average American household, many of whom may have visited Yellowstone Park in a recent summer.

The anti-hunting groups assigned staff full-time to the issue and sent them to locations around the park. These groups fed emotion laden stories and footage daily to the Denver offices of the major television networks. Coverage was almost constant on prime time news. Emotions ran high and FWP got letters from concerned citizens all across the nation as well as from other countries, from as far away as Germany. The emotional press coverage was overwhelmingly negative for FWP and for hunters in general.

FWP responded to this media crisis as most state fish and wildlife agencies filled with scientists and facts would have responded. There were fact sheets sent to the press and news releases sent out on a regular basis.

When the press would appear at the FWP offices, the agency spokesperson was filmed as a "talking head" giving the facts and logic behind the situation. The science behind the situation indicated that killing the bison was the correct action to take.

The problem was that FWP only appeared as a "talking head" on video, spouting facts and science. FWP's emotional impact on public opinion nationwide was minimal. On a daily basis, the anti-hunting groups submitted graphic, emotion-laden footage to the major television networks showing bison being killed, skinned, and eviscerated. These groups needed little newscaster commentary to get the desired public reaction. The anti-hunting groups were well aware that emotion was a powerful tool for communicating their message.

The summer after the season of the bison media frenzy, I attended the first Governor's Hunting Heritage Symposium at Big Sky, Montana, along with several FWP staff. One of the symposium speakers, Roger O'Neil, was the bureau chief and a correspondent for NBC News in Denver, Colorado. He spoke about the bison issue and the press coverage by his network. He likened the anti-hunting groups to having a Ph.D. in how to work with the media, daily suggesting stories and providing material for their side of the issue.

The news anchor then likened FWP to having a grade school level understanding of working with the media. FWP would respond only when contacted by the network and was not aggressive in feeding material and story suggestions to them (O'Neil pers. comm.). Obviously, the FWP employees had their routine press issues to attend to and could not focus on just the bison issue, while the anti-hunting groups devoted staff full time to just this one issue. Worse, FWP's efforts focused only on addressing people's prefrontal lobes with logic and facts, while the anti-hunting groups focused on addressing people's limbic systems and emotions.

Another important point from this example is that agencies need to proactively build good relationships with the media. In the Montana case, good relationships had been built with many local media within the state, but when the issue went national, there was no existing network of relations with national media. Unfortunately, the agency did not successfully build these relations. There seemed to be a pervasive view, at least among the agency employees I knew, that the national media should be avoided whenever possible in hopes that this would allow the controversy to subside.

The whole concept of appealing to people's emotions as well as their logic was summed up very succinctly in a conversation I had years later with Jim Fowler, the well-known television personality from the show *Wild Kingdom*. Jim (J. Fowler pers. comm.) described television as "A great medium that can make people feel but it can't make them think!" Consider this statement when communicating through the medium of television. Sound bites do not communicate factual arguments well. Television is a visual medium that can effectively elicit emotions. So plan to use visual images to generate the desired emotions whenever producing information for television.

Visual Portrayal is Critical in Creating Emotion

Electronic and print media of all types historically have been used to promote specific points of view. You need only look at newspaper accounts in the U.S. during the mid-1800s related to such issues as political campaigns, Native American policies, and numerous other topics to find evidence of biases in the media. As a more current example, one could make the case that television's Fox News channel is very pro conservative while CNN's news channel is very pro liberal.

The same potential for bias is present when the media deals with wildlife issues. The proliferation of visual media through film and television has enhanced the art of using visual images to subtly elicit specific, strong emotions and promote a particular bias while professing impartiality. An example of using television visual images to subtly influence the public is cited below to demonstrate the powerful effects images can have in creating emotions.

A CASE EXAMPLE: DOCUMENTARY DEBACLE

During the late 1970s, I was working on my doctorate degree in wildlife science at Colorado State University. One of my courses dealt with uses of public media and public presentations. Graduate students in this course analyzed a broadcast from the weekly television newsmagazine *60 Minutes*, a CBS show that launched in 1968. The broadcast chosen for analysis was entitled "The Guns of Autumn" and focused on hunting in America. CBS presented this broadcast as a documentary piece and all of us watched as noted newscaster, Dan Rather, hosted.

At the conclusion of the class analysis of this broadcast, all of us graduate students arrived at the unanimous conclusion that the broadcast was extremely biased and portrayed a strong anti-hunting view. How could a major media outlet documentary pull this off while claiming it was a "fair" presentation of the hunting issue?

A detailed examination of the broadcast by our class and professor revealed numerous examples of biased portrayals through selections of the visual footage for the broadcast. As an example, the apparent fairness of equal time for representatives of both pro-hunting and anti-hunting views was really affected by clever manipulation of emotion by using visual imagery.

The anti-hunting viewpoint was portrayed using Cleveland Amory, a prominent anti-hunting spokesperson at that time. His scene was shot in a library with neatly shelved books as a backdrop (sending the subtle message of learning and wise ideas). Mr. Amory was nattily dressed in a casual sweater as a "Mr. Rogers" type who spoke eloquently about his anti-hunting views. Now, cut to the film footage portraying the pro-hunting viewpoint. CBS used visuals of a group of blue-collar "bubba" types in a parking lot at night with the neon sign of a beer hall as a backdrop. This may have been equal time, but it surely used the power of visual cues to slant the image and the emotions evoked in order to influence the public.

A CASE EXAMPLE: THE PRESIDENT'S PHOTO OPS

Years later when I was working for the Montana Department of Fish, Wildlife & Parks, there was a meeting of upper management where a guest speaker gave a presentation about use of television to evoke emotion and present a specific point of view. The speaker was a newscaster in Washington, D.C., during the Reagan administration.

This newscaster was incensed about how President Reagan's press secretary manipulated the media reporters by staging the images the press was allowed to take and the scenes permitted for filming. The press secretary accomplished this by positioning the press group in specific areas so that they could only get particular shots with specific backgrounds.

An example given by this speaker was June 6, 1984, when Ronald Reagan gave a speech at Omaha Beach commemorating the fortieth anniversary of the landing of American troops there on D-Day during World War II.

The press was positioned so that the only shots they could get were of Ronald Reagan speaking with Omaha Beach as the background. The point was that a day after the speech no one would remember what President Reagan said—all that would be remembered was the president with Omaha Beach as a background. The idea that a picture is worth a thousand words is really true and the Regan press secretary knew that! President Reagan also knew this from his many years as a film star. Staging occurred at every Reagan photo and filming opportunity.

The newscaster told us that she finally became so frustrated with this "manipulation" that she decided to do a piece on it during their nightly television broadcast. During that broadcast, the newscaster elaborated extensively on how the Reagan administration was interfering with the media's objective reporting.

That evening, after the broadcast, the reporter was at home when she got a call from Reagan's press secretary. When the reporter answered her phone the press secretary said, "Saw your broadcast tonight. Nice piece. But nobody will listen." Then the press secretary hung up. The reporter was momentarily stunned then realized the press secretary was right! The reporter had been a "talking head" on screen and there were no photos or visual footage to make the piece memorable.

How does this apply to your agency? First, remember that the visual image for any media and especially television is critical. And don't forget the "talking head" should be avoided where possible. You can always find something to make the footage visually impactful. What about animals? They're always great and you work for people who can get them to you. Holding a bear cub, an eagle, or any wild animal is one way to portray a caring attitude for wildlife and its management. At the very least, you can use stock wildlife footage or a scenic background of wildlife habitat with dramatic sunlight and shadows.

Too many times agencies fall into the trap of letting their technical and audiovisual folks make all these decisions when it comes to filming or photographing something for release to the public. My experience suggests that the audiovisual staff is primarily concerned with the technical aspects of camera operation, use of any artificial lights, sound volume and clarity, and how easily the job of recording the footage can be accomplished. It is typical for them to set up their equipment in an office or meeting room at the agency, bring in the director or whoever is going to be on camera, and then shoot footage of them talking. Many of these technical experts do not appreciate the need for really impactful footage. They just go for the facts as spoken on camera. Remember that your audiovisual experts are usually **technical** experts, not **communication** experts!

Sometimes it is the director or speaker presenting the message who is not aware of the need for impactful imagery and they want to just get it over with. It seems too vain to fuss about how things look. The agency's chief of communication, if a strategist, would be a strong ally here to ensure that full use is made of imagery as a powerful tool.

As I've said before, a picture really is worth a thousand words. So when filming, you may want to keep in mind that you're using a medium that has been perfected by the entertainment industry. That industry has many people whose specific job is to ensure that the "look" of the footage is correct for the desired effect. Why should a fish and wildlife agency do less when providing footage to television stations or photos to print media?

Use Professional Information and Education Agency Staff

Most wildlife issues do not reach the magnitude of national attention that the bison issue did in Montana, but this does not lessen the need for good relations with the media. Too often, high-level biologists or wardens single-handedly provide information for major media coverage without any assistance from professional communication staff within their own agency. The assumption is that because employees such as the chief of wildlife or enforcement know the facts best, they should be the ones to communicate to the public.

Enhanced relations between an agency's biologists, enforcement staff, and the agency's information and education (I&E) staff will help immensely with effective communication to the publics. Of course, this premise depends on fish and wildlife agencies hiring professional I&E

people trained in communication and public relations, as opposed to hiring or promoting staff members without such training.

Historically, I have observed in many state fish and wildlife agencies what I believe is a bias of those from the "hard, physical sciences" such as biology and chemistry against those with training in the "softer sciences" such as psychology, human dimensions, information, education, and communication. This bias seems to be one of those mostly unspoken parts of a fish and wildlife agency's culture. Those with hard science backgrounds appear to see those with soft science backgrounds as less credible. In these situations, full appreciation and understanding of the art and science of communication is lacking. The old saying, *you don't appreciate what you don't understand*, seems true in this instance.

All agency staff can benefit from increasing their understanding of the art and science of public relations and communication. It is becoming more critical as the information highway expands through electronic communications and social media. The days are past when agencies were trusted by their public to do the right thing because those agencies had the trained experts. Now self-proclaimed experts abound.

Everyone is an Expert

The proliferation of self-proclaimed experts is demonstrated in an anecdote told to me by a western state fish and wildlife employee. It was purported as fact, but I wonder if it isn't an urban legend? Regardless, the point is still valid.

A local wildlife biologist had called a meeting one night in a small western town to discuss proposed deer hunting regulations for the surrounding area. The meeting room was full, and the atmosphere was good-humored since all the locals knew each other.

During the meeting, Joe, one of the local townspeople, took issue with a particular regulation that increased the doe harvest. Joe expounded for quite some time on his observations from many years of deer hunting and proclaimed to know for sure that the deer numbers were down and that the doe harvest regulation was bad! Joe exclaimed that his years of hunting experience and the fact that he had lived here his whole life were a better basis than any college-trained biologist machinations for assessing the deer situation.

After Joe made his prolonged and passionate plea to the crowd of onlookers the biologist gave his reply.

"Joe, you are the plumber who owns the business down the street, right?"

"That's right, and I'm the best at it too," Joe answered proudly.

"I don't doubt that. However, I've flushed a toilet for over forty years and I don't consider myself a plumber."

The crowd roared with laughter and Joe himself had to allow a slow grin. This anecdote illustrates two points: 1) that many people consider themselves experts, and 2) the appropriate reading of a situation and the appropriate use of emotion (humor in this case) can help immensely in communication and credibility.

Communication When Handling Misconduct or the Perception of Misconduct

Not only is skill in using visual media important, but the entire art and science of communication is critical when dealing with the public and the media. These skills are never of greater consequence than when dealing with public perceptions of agency misconduct, whether it is misconduct of the entire agency or one individual.

Those in power sometimes forget this. As author and professor of leadership and organizational psychology Ronald Riggio (2011) writes, "Although many leaders start out using their power to get things done and to benefit others, over time they may begin to believe that whatever they do is right (and they delude themselves into thinking that benefiting others is their primary concern)." Philosopher Terry Price says that, over time, powerful people may begin to believe that they are "above the law" and that the rules that apply to others do not apply to them. Price refers to this as "exception-making."

Moreover, followers of the authority figure may collude with the leader. For example, they look the other way when the leader misbehaves. They may even believe that the misbehavior is okay because of the leader's authority and power (Price 2005).

What follows are four examples of misconduct, how they were handled, and the consequences of the actions taken. These are actual events that I learned about during my career in natural resources.

CASE EXAMPLE #1: BOB'S FISHING LICENSE

One high-ranking public agency individual was acting as the director of the agency while a search was being made to fill the position. All indications were that this person would be selected to serve as the director after the search was completed. This person, (I'll call him Bob) was spending a weekend afternoon fishing on a local lake with his girlfriend. A retired game warden had recognized Bob in his boat, and as the retired game warden was driving down the access road leaving the lake, he met a new, young warden going to the lake to check licenses. The retiree decided to have some fun and told the young warden that he had spotted a nefarious looking character on the lake and then gave a description of Bob and Bob's boat and girlfriend.

The new warden, anxious to do a good job, drove to the lake and launched his own boat. Soon the warden spotted Bob and Bob's girlfriend in their boat. Motoring over, the young warden eased his boat alongside Bob's and then recognized that it was the acting director for his own agency. The warden realized that the retiree had played a joke on him. The young warden chatted amicably for a while, and then prepared to leave. At this moment Bob's girlfriend spoke up and said, "Aren't you going to check our fishing licenses?"

The warden stopped and said, "I'm sure you are both legally licensed, but since I am here I will go ahead and check you licenses anyway." The woman produced her license and the warden found it in order. Bob fumbled around in his wallet and tackle box but could not find his license. The truth was that Bob had forgotten to buy a license and realized his mistake only when checked by the warden. This, in itself, was only a minor failure and would have probably resulted in a warning ticket with no real consequences other than a lot of ribbing by folks back at the agency.

Bob, however, chose to try and cover up his innocent mistake. Bob asked the warden to allow him to send him a copy of the missing license once Bob had returned home and had a chance to "find" it. The friendly game warden agreed to have Bob send in a copy of his license on Monday morning.

Bob had created a real problem for himself. Bob knew that if he immediately went to town and purchased a license that the license would reveal the date and time of purchase and it would become obvious that Bob had no license when checked by the warden. So Bob chose to handle it alone. Bob further complicated matters by his actions when returning to work on Monday morning. Bob got a file copy of someone else's license and forged his information onto the license and made a copy of the document and faxed it to the warden.

When the warden compared the license number on the license faxed from Bob with agency records, it became clear what Bob had done. Now Bob had complicated his initial innocent mistake by attempting to hide it and committing a much more grievous offense of cover up. When the truth became known, Bob was eliminated from consideration for the agency director position. All who knew of this incident believed that Bob could have overcome his innocent mistake and become the agency director if he had just confessed his mistake. But his attempt at a cover up was not excusable.

CASE EXAMPLE #2: LARRY'S DUI

Compare Bob's example with another public agency director's story. This occurred when the director (I'll call him Larry) had been out driving a state car one night. Larry had a few too many drinks with dinner and crashed the state car. When the police arrived, the director was arrested for driving under the influence (DUI). The director was hospitalized for his injuries, but he faced a future court appearance. Most disturbing was that the press would view the police reports the following day as a normal part of reporters searching for news. Larry's DUI would become public knowledge in less than twenty-four hours.

Larry knew that he was in big trouble and could be fired. From his hospital bed the next morning, he called together his professional communications staff and explained what had happened. He asked his staff for advice on how he should handle the incident publicly. His communications staff sympathized with him and told him that he must do two things. First, was to "get out in front" of the story and get his version in the press before the information hit the newswires. Second, was that he had to confess to his wrongdoing and ask his superiors and the public for forgiveness as well as communicate what he was going to do to resolve the problem.

To the director's credit, he took the advice from his communications staff and immediately informed his superiors of the incident, then called a press conference. At this press conference, Larry admitted to driving after drinking too much. He also confessed that he had "a problem" and that he was going to join a program for alcoholics and get help. While all this made good news, Larry's actions immediately following the accident were the kind that all reasonable people could accept. The result was that his staff, his boss, and the public forgave Larry. He was true to his word, sought treatment, and remained director for a number of years after this incident had become ancient history.

CASE EXAMPLE #3: SAM'S TRIP

A wealthy commissioner for a state conservation agency asked the agency director (I'll call him Sam) and another high-ranking agency staff person to accompany him on an all-expense paid trip to Africa. It was the commissioner's treat to recognize two hard-working staff. This was to be a hunting expedition where Sam and his staff person would also have the chance to view wildlife management practices in another country. So far, no problem—just a once-in-a-lifetime opportunity.

Due to the opportunity to professionally observe another country's conservation programs, the agency director and his staff person reasoned that it would be okay to buy some of the needed items for the trip using agency funds. They bought hunting boots, clothing, binoculars, etc. These items would be put into the agency warehouse for other agency employee use once the trip to Africa was completed. Thus, Sam and his staff person were receiving no permanent benefit of the expenditure of the agency funds.

Do you see any problem here? While the rationale could be justified and a case made for these actions, what the director and his staff person did not consider was how the general public might view this type of decision. That is something the agency communications professionals would have likely perceived immediately had they been asked.

The purchases of hunting boots and other equipment were made and the trip to Africa was taken. All this was done with a clear conscience and no ill intent on the part of Sam, his staff person, or the commissioner. But when Sam returned to the United States from Africa, the press got wind of this junket, and upon finding out public agency funds were used to buy some of the equipment, the headlines in the press screamed "Misuse of Funds!"

Sam, the high-ranking staffer, and the commissioner gave their rationale and explained that there was no wrongdoing. It seemed perfectly logical to them. However, public opinion turned against Sam and his two companions. They were castigated in numerous news stories, and eventually the agency's publics joined forces with the press in calling for the resignation of all three.

In this case, the public's perception of wrongdoing was enough to cost these people their reputations and their jobs. In fact, a strong case could be made that there was not even any real wrongdoing. The point is to always consider the potential public impressions of your actions. **The fact that actions are not illegal is often insufficient to pass the test of public perceptions of wrongdoing.**

CASE EXAMPLE #4: DOUG'S TURKEY HUNT

This last example illustrates how doing the hard thing, even when not required, is often the right decision regarding public perception. A retired fish and wildlife agency director related this story to me. When he was an active director, he had hosted a spring turkey hunt with a group of friends that included a neighboring state fish and wildlife agency director (I'll call him Doug). During a morning hunt, Doug accidently shot a hen turkey. Hens are illegal in spring seasons; only gobblers are legal. Doug returned to camp with the hen in hand and confessed his mistake.

Following protocol, the host state director called the local game warden and asked him to come and investigate the breaking of the game law. The warden arrived, talked to Doug, and confiscated the turkey. Doug was truthful and with great candor explained his mistake. The warden issued Doug a warning ticket that carried no penalty or fine.

The host director stood off to the side observing these proceedings and then approached the warden who worked for him. He told the warden that he had performed correctly and followed all legal protocols for the situation. Then he asked the warden to issue a paying ticket to Doug. This ticket carried the penalty of a stiff fine for breaking the law. Doug was first upset over this request, but the warden did as told and issued a paying ticket.

It was neither easy nor required for the host director to request a fine be levied against his friend, but it was the right decision. The host director demonstrated exceptional communication awareness of potential public perceptions when he required a paying ticket. He explained to Doug that if word got out that Doug had killed a hen turkey illegally and had received only a warning, then there'd be the very real risk of the public's perceiving this as favoritism and special privilege due to Doug's position as director of a neighboring state wildlife agency. After reflecting on this, Doug told the host director that he appreciated his wisdom in this matter and he gladly paid the fine.

Analysis

What can we learn from these experiences? The most obvious is that truth is always better than fiction. Covering up a mistake seldom works and forever after puts the guilty party in fear of discovery. Bob's mistake was minor and due to nothing more than a small error of forgetting to buy a fishing license. He compounded his mistake by a cover up that was unforgiveable. He lost his opportunity to become director of a state agency.

The much worse mistake of Larry (DUI while driving a state vehicle) was overcome by honest admission to the mistake, getting in front of the story, and communicating a plan of how Larry was going to fix the problem. Due to following these hard but simple steps, Larry was able to overcome his mistake completely. The principle here is to make the infraction a one-day media story by telling the whole story at the first opportunity, rather than dribbling it out over a series of days or in response to a series of reporters' calls.

The story of Sam's Africa trip illustrates that while you may not actually be doing something illegal, it's all about public perception. Sam could justify buying hunting equipment because it was going to be turned over to the agency when Sam was finished with it. But the power of public perception ruled.

Doug's accidental shooting of a hen turkey was actually cleared by an enforcement officer who only wrote him a warning ticket. But such events must be handled with sensitivity to how they will be perceived by the public. In Doug's example, his host director was sensitive to this principle and ensured that Doug would not risk any negative publicity regarding the way the incident was handled. The bottom line is that fish and wildlife agencies need to use the assistance of their professional communication staff when dealing with the media and the public. Forging ahead single-handedly is fraught with danger.

Summary

Wildlife scientists typically ignore consideration of emotion in working with the media, the public, or in making decisions affecting wildlife. While this is a correct approach in conducting research, it does not mean that emotion should be ignored when communicating with publics. Wildlife science and the science of communication are two different things!

The fact that people make decisions in the emotional center of the brain means that if we want to communicate to influence decisions, then we need to address the emotional part of the brain. Using facts and logic alone is insufficient. Starting messages with our "why" is one way to create messages for our publics that addresses values and emotions. Too often our agency messages focus solely on the "what" and the "how," which is all facts and logic-based information.

Visual media is prevalent in today's society. Knowing how to use visual cues is a science in itself that has been perfected by the television and movie industries. We would do well to learn the importance of this tool. Most agencies have professional communication staff. It is critical to recognize the contribution they can make to the agency and use these professional staff accordingly.

Sometimes there are slip-ups or actual wrongdoing by agency employees. The higher in the agency's hierarchy these events occur, the more likely that public attention will be focused on the agency. How these events are handled is crucial.

If wrongdoing has occurred, then the agency wrongdoer must get in front of the story by going to the press and telling all. Do not drag it out by leaking a little more public information each day. After admitting the mistake, ask for forgiveness and explain what will be done to prevent this kind of mistake in the future. This is the hardest road to follow when you are the one in the wrong, but it is the only way to clear your record.

So far I have addressed a number of tools and concepts for managing and leading an agency. These have been gleaned from over twenty-five years of my professional life working with state fish and wildlife agencies. The next chapter is entitled "A Look Ahead" and addresses some of the challenges I see for our profession in the near future. Using the tools and concepts in this book will help us to address these hard challenges affecting the very survival of our natural resource profession.

Literature Cited

Geist, Valerius. 2013. "Disinterested Science." *Fair Chase*. Winter issue Vol. 28 (4). Boone and Crockett Club. Missoula, MT.

Price, Terry. 2005. *The Allure of Toxic Leaders*. Oxford University Press. New York, NY.

Riggio, Ronald E. 2011. "Why Powerful People Break Laws and Misbehave: Understanding Why Leaders Become Intoxicated by Power." Nov. 13. *Psychology Today* at psychologytoday.com.

Sinek, Simon. 2009. *Start with Why*. The Penguin Group. New York, NY. 248 pp.

Chapter Seven

A Look Ahead

In this chapter I am going to offer my views on some changes I believe are affecting the wildlife profession and the challenges they present for state fish and wildlife agencies. I had the privilege of working with numerous agencies across the nation for the last quarter of a century, allowing me to develop a broad, national perspective. In addition, the forty-two years I've been involved with the wildlife profession as a certified wildlife biologist have provided me a long-view perspective that takes into account the many changes that have occurred over that time and the influences that brought them about.

For better of worse, we are all the result of our experiences. My experiences over the last forty-two years as a professional wildlife biologist and over the last fifty-five years as a hunter and angler have shaped my views and my expectations for the future of wildlife management. I don't see my personal hunting and fishing experiences as unusual. In fact, I believe that most of my experiences are representative of a large majority of people who hunt and fish. I will share some of my personal experiences as a way to provide some background for the opinions I express in this chapter.

The Changes in Private Land Access

I conducted my Ph.D. research on hunting access issues with private lands in Colorado during the late 1970s. My findings were that private lands were closing at an increasing rate. Reasons for closure were many, but control by the landowner was primary at that time (Guynn 1979). My observations are that the closure of private lands has continued to increase across the nation since then although I believe financial gains plays a larger role in today's closures. The impact of the accumulated loss of access signifies a major change for hunters in reduced opportunities, increased costs to access private lands, and more crowded conditions on public lands.

Shelby and his co-authors (1983) speculate that recreational boaters' perceptions of crowding are influenced by the amount of crowding that existed during the person's initial exposure to the recreational experience. It is possible that older hunters with many years of experience similarly base their expectations and preferences for a hunting experience on their initial experiences from many years ago when there was more private land with free access and less crowding.

If Shelby's speculations apply to hunters, then younger hunters' initial experiences in more recent years may make them more tolerant of crowding because that was part of their initial experience. Yet today, seventy-three percent of hunters in the United States are not young hunters—they are thirty-five years old or older, and fifty-five percent are older than age forty-five (U.S. Dept. Interior, et al. 2011). Because these hunters' initial experiences were likely twenty to forty years ago, in a much less crowded situation, I believe current crowding is a major factor for most hunters and will continue to be so for a number of years to come. Generational amnesia has yet to occur for most of those hunting today.

Also, a major difference between boating or other non-consumptive recreation experiences and the consumptive recreational pursuits such as hunting is that the non-consumptive experiences are not nearly as competitive as hunting or even fishing. When enjoying camping, outdoor scenery, bird watching, or other such activities, the fact that others may be doing the same thing in close proximity is not nearly as disruptive as when stalking a big-game animal or calling a spring gobbler.

I present here some of my personal experiences over an extended period of time in order to put the concepts of crowding and loss of access into perspective. The following paragraphs offer similar experiences for several different types of hunting.

PHEASANT HUNTING ACCESS

Pheasant hunting in the Midwest is a favorite sport of many. I began traveling to south-central Nebraska in 1972 to pheasant hunt. At that time, my hunting companions and I hunted on 2,000 acres owned by a farm family whom we paid for providing our food and lodging. We also hunted many other properties in the vicinity of that farm over the years, and during our first decade of hunting we were turned down only once when asking permission to access the other properties. We returned to hunt pheasants on those properties each year for over thirty years.

As the years progressed, however, my hunting companions and I began to notice posted signs appearing along the rural section roads. By the late 1980s, it was as common to be refused permission to hunt as to be granted the privilege. By the mid-1990s, there were few places that could be accessed by just requesting permission. Posted signs had become prevalent. My hunting partners and I began seeing many signs stating private landholdings were now leased by hunting outfitter services. Finally, the last two years I pheasant hunted in Nebraska (2010 and 2011), the only property available to for us to hunt was the original 2,000 acres that belonged to the farm family where we began hunting in 1972. I have stopped pheasant hunting in Nebraska due to the closure of the many properties I used to hunt.

ELK HUNTING ACCESS

This continued closure of private lands is not restricted to pheasant hunting. Between 1986 and 1996, I worked for the Montana Department of Fish, Wildlife & Parks, and I witnessed the phenomena of increasing private land closures to elk hunting. I was surprised upon scouring the hunting statistics in Montana to find that during the 1950s, elk hunting success rates were around fifty percent! Current success rates are more in the neighborhood of twenty percent at best. What happened? There are more elk in Montana now than in the 1950s, and hunter numbers within the state had not increased that much. The state still had a human population of only around one million. For years, the legislature had curtailed the number of nonresident licenses to 17,500. What was going on?

Increasing closures of private lands was what was happening! More lands were being leased and closed to the public, and nonresidents were buying more large ranches for personal hunting opportunities. As mentioned in previous chapers, the issue of access to private lands for hunting had become so acute in Montana that by 1993, the legislature passed a joint resolution requesting Governor Marc Racicot to appoint a blue-ribbon panel to address the issue (Guynn 1997).

The mobility of elk was a factor that further exacerbated the access issue in Montana. In contrast to white-tailed deer, elk will move great distances and often exhibit annual migrations. Studies by Montana Fish, Wildlife & Parks biologists Ken Hamlin and Julie Cunningham found that elk were moving off of public lands with high hunting pressure and onto less pressured private lands.

These movements were learned behaviors that occurred as much as a week before hunting season opened (Ken Hamlin pers. comm.). The September-October issue of *Montana Outdoors* in 2014 quoted Julie Cunningham saying, "the main driver [of reduced hunting access] seems to be the massive change in land ownership starting in the mid-1990s. . . it went from working ranches owned by people that usually allowed public hunting to 'amenity' ranches owned by people who did not want public hunting. It's not surprising that elk have figured out that the best place to spend the hunting season is where hunters are not allowed" (Dickson 2014).

My conversations with other biologists in Idaho (Toby Boudreau pers. comm.) and Colorado (Jim Satterfield pers. comm.) confirm that these states also are experiencing the same type of phenomena with elk hunting access.

TURKEY HUNTING ACCESS

This movement of game animals from public lands onto less pressured private lands does not seem to be confined to elk. A recent study in Louisiana using GPS tracking devices showed a turkey gobbler moving off a public wildlife management area onto private land as soon as hunting season arrived and staying there until the end of the season (Nickens 2014).

My personal experience with turkey hunting is illustrated by the following two examples from Nebraska and Montana. During the late 1970s, I began hunting spring turkeys on public lands around Chadron, Nebraska, in the northwest corner of that state. The hunting pressure was minimal and the success of my hunting partners and I was very good. I continued to hunt this area for the next thirty-plus years and watched hunting pressure gradually increase and the hunting success of my friends and I suffer accordingly. The last four years I hunted that area, I failed to get any chance to harvest a bird, but I always saw lots of other hunters. I no longer hunt there.

While living in Montana between 1986 and 1996, I searched for places to hunt spring turkeys. I acquired permission to hunt on a ranch in central Montana and had great hunting experiences there for two years. Then the ranch was sold and the new landowner no longer granted hunting access. I immediately began searching for another ranch to hunt turkeys, and after several years received permission to hunt spring turkeys on a ranch near Roundup, Montana. A friend and I had a great hunt there, but by the next year that ranch had also been sold and the new landowner did not grant permission to hunt. I was not able to find a new place to hunt turkeys on private land without paying a steep access fee. My Montana turkey hunts in 2015 and 2016 cost $1,200 each for an unguided three-day hunt on private land. I currently do not hunt turkeys in Montana anymore.

DEER HUNTING ACCESS
Many hunters may consider hunting access for pheasants, elk, and turkeys to be important, but nationally, more people pursue white-tailed deer than any other big-game species (Adams and Ross 2015). The common mantra among white-tailed deer hunting industry experts touts sneaking into the hunting area undetected. The accepted theory is that hunting pressure causes bucks to move off the property, seek dense cover, and/or to become nocturnal. The implication is that the more land available to hunt and the less hunting pressure on that land, the better the hunting. In other words, properties with very limited access are best!

I believe that my deer hunting experiences from 1999 to 2013 while living in West Virginia are quite common. When I moved to a West Virginia rural community in 1999, I had permission to hunt several hundred acres of whitetail habitat on a farm adjoining my five acres of land. Over time, the majority of that farm was leased to other deer hunters and I lost hunting privileges there. By 2011, I was relegated to deer hunting on twenty acres that adjoined my back fence. Then in 2012, those twenty acres were sold to someone for their own hunting pleasure. In the space of fourteen years, I went from several hundred acres of land available to deer hunt to zero.

I could continue with more of my personal experiences throughout the last fifty-five years, but I think John Gierach (2015) summed up the hunter's access dilemma and resignation well when he wrote about crowding:

> Nothing lasts forever, and after a while you start waiting for the other shoe to drop. . . The days when you could think of the natural world as immutable may well be coming to an end. . .

Hunters are crowded onto public lands, or have to either buy or lease lands, or quit hunting altogether when private lands are closed to hunting. The crowding of hunters onto public lands decreases the quality of hunting and reduces success for most hunters. These decreases are due not only to exceeding crowding tolerances of individual hunters, but also because game animals react to crowding by either leaving highly pressured properties, becoming more nocturnal, or otherwise adapting, all of which reduce hunting success on public lands.

A Systems View of the Hunting Access Issue

Complex problems seldom have simple answers. Hunting access is part of a system of interactions each with causes and effects. The following systems diagram is based upon systems concepts defined by Peter Senge (1990) and includes a number of the causes and effects related to hunting.

View the circles in the diagram as cogs in the system. Where the cogs touch, they interact and influence each other's movement. For simplicity I have limited the factors interacting in this drawing to nine. I'm sure that many other cogs could be added. Each cog is underlined in the text below.

High game numbers – There is no question that today we enjoy high numbers of big-game animals that could only be dreamt about in 1900. Wildlife management in the United States has succeeded to the point that it is the model for the rest of the world. This success, coupled with a growing human population, has been largely responsible for an increase in hunter numbers since the early 1900s. It is only in the last few decades that the hunter numbers have experienced any real declines from all time highs.

Pressure on all hunting lands (both private and public) has increased as the number of hunters has soared. **Loss of habitat** has also contributed to increasing pressure on the remaining lands supporting wildlife.

Increased closure and leasing of hunting lands – As the pressure on all hunting lands increases, several things happen. While a landowner may have been willing to grant hunting access to a small number of hunters during a season, as the number of hunters increases, the landowner is less inclined to deal with the incoming tide of requests for permission to hunt. Private land access closures increase.

In addition, hunters and outfitters seek out private lands with good hunting to lease for their exclusive use. This causes **increased pressure and crowding on public lands** as more hunters are forced off private lands and onto remaining public lands. As the public land experience begins to suffer from this crowding, more hunters (who can afford it) begin to **lease or purchase lands for personal recreation.** This has the effect of perpetuating and accelerating the cycle.

System of Interactions Affecting Hunting

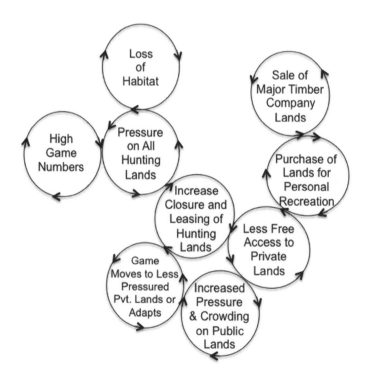

The leasing or purchasing of private land is also influenced by the fact that most **major timber companies like WESTVACO, Weyerhaeuser, Georgia Pacific, and International Paper are all divesting themselves of timber lands** (Gary Youngblood pers. comm.) These timberlands were once mostly available to public hunting, but now public access has greatly diminished and I expect that it will continue to do so on these former timber company lands.

As crowding and hunting pressure mounts on public lands, **game species adapt to the increased hunting pressure (e.g., become more nocturnal, etc.), thus making hunting public lands less successful. Those game species without an affinity to a small core area move to less pressured private lands.** This only exacerbates the **increasing leasing and closures and of private lands.**

Leasing and purchasing of hunting properties becomes a basic matter of economics. As hunting access decreases and the quality of hunting on private lands increases, the quality of hunting and success on public lands decreases. Thus, demand for hunting on those private lands increases. We all learned in economics 101 that as supply decreases and demand increases, the cost increases. Thus, leasing and paying for access has increased significantly over time and continues to do so.

CONSEQUENCES OF THE CHANGES
IN PRIVATE LAND ACCESS STATUS

I believe that this system of interactions is a major influence on hunting in America today. I believe that these interactions also are a major contributor to the low numbers of hunters nationally as only 4.4 percent of the total population now hunts (U.S. Dept. Interior, et. al. 2011). As far as introducing youth to the sport, it is much more difficult to take along a son or daughter when it costs $3,000 to $10,000 to take them on a deer or elk hunt.

Most assuredly, we have become a more urbanized society, and that is often assumed to be a major influence contributing to low hunter numbers. But that simple concept deserves greater exploration. I believe that the significance of urban or rural residency impacts **access for hunting** and that this is at least as relevant to explaining low hunter numbers.

If you have no place to hunt, then it doesn't matter where you live. The numerous surveys of hunters' reasons for dropping out of hunting list such motives as "not enough time," "busy with other activities," and "loss of interest." I believe that reduced access influences all of these. If major travel is required to reach accessible hunting lands, then "not enough time" is a factor! If the quality of the hunting experience has declined through crowding of public lands and lower success due to game adapting to crowding, then the result is "loss of interest" and "busy with other activities." The preceding illustration shows generally how an individual's rural or urban residency influences their amount of access for hunting.

Interactions of Hunting Access and Urban/Rural Residence

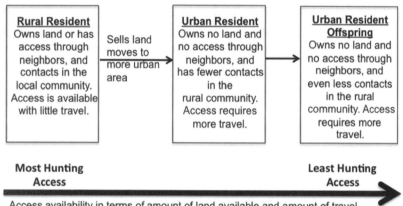

Access availability in terms of amount of land available and amount of travel required to reach accessible lands

Nationally, the big-game hunter numbers have remained stagnant over the decade between 2001 and 2011 (U.S. Dept. Interior et al. 2011). Archery hunting, however, has bucked that trend by showing increases in participation (Duda and Bissell 2000). I believe that the increase in archery hunting in recent years has been largely a result of many hunters seeking less crowded hunting opportunities outside the general gun season, which is the hunting season that generally experiences the most crowding.

Nationally, the issue of access to private lands for hunting has become critical, and so far state fish and wildlife agencies have been unable to significantly influence this alarming trend. These agencies manage wildlife populations through hunting regulations. They focus most of their attention on surveying animal numbers, monitoring the influence of their regulations on wildlife populations, and enforcing those regulations. Through the regulatory process, hunters are managed as to when and how much they can hunt. According to Bullock (2015), "Approximately 1.42 billion acres or 73 percent of all land in the United States is privately owned." State fish and wildlife agencies, however, have little control over hunting access to these private lands.

While there are some publicly accessible state wildlife management areas and other state-controlled lands, overall this amounts to less than two percent of the land within any state. Therefore, it is impossible for a state fish and wildlife agency to own enough land to effectively impact the hunting access issue.

Federally owned lands can make up a greater portion of some states, particularly in the western part of the country. A few states such as Alaska and Nevada are composed of a majority of federally owned lands. But this is the exception rather than the norm when considering all fifty states. Finding a solution to the access problem for private lands will require working with both landowners and hunters in an adaptive leadership effort.

Many states have implemented some type of hunting access program in response to the growing problems associated with access to lands for public hunting. These programs seek to open private lands through various arrangements with landowners. For example, the Montana Department of Fish, Wildlife & Parks makes outright payments to landowners who enroll in a block management program to provide public hunting access. Colorado's Department of Parks and Wildlife has a Ranching for Wildlife program where landowners receive big-game tags that they can sell as long as the landowner conducts some modicum of wildlife habitat management and provides a very limited amount of public access.

A number of nongovernmental organizations such as the Rocky Mountain Elk Foundation and Pheasants Forever have implemented access programs also. Many other programs have been tried over the last thirty years, but the reality is that, while these types of programs help to some extent, they have not been able to solve the growing problem of access. Remember that a telling indicator of an adaptive issue is that the problem continues to persist in spite of many efforts at solution.

Changes in Fishing Recreation

Since I am a wildlife biologist, my experiences and research in fishing are not nearly as extensive as wildlife. I will offer only a few initial impressions that may or may not be accurate in a national perspective.

I will limit myself to three examples: one in the East and two in the Rocky Mountains. I grew up fishing the New River in Virginia for warmwater species such as smallmouth bass and bluegill. I fished stretches of the river between Radford and Narrows, Virginia, a distance of about forty river miles. I began fishing there when I was in high school during the 1960s, and I continued to fish there until 2010. Over this half-century, I observed fishing pressure slowly increase.

Initially, it was not uncommon during a day of fishing to see only one or two other boats or actually seem to be the only boat on the river. My last several years of fishing the New River, I experienced numerous other boats on the river, and often I had to float a stretch of water near the bank behind other boats fishing the same waters.

During the last half-century, the Virginia Department of Game and Inland Fisheries has purchased a public boat launch at Pepper's Ferry and one at Whitethorn. The boat launch at Pepper's Ferry, near Radford, now has numerous boats launching daily and often scuba divers working the area as well as a dozen or more people canoeing, kayaking, camping, and enjoying the river. This has been a boon of access for the public and a good thing. The downside is that fishing pressure has increased dramatically. My fishing success has taken a consequential nosedive. I don't cherish fishing the New River like I once did.

The second example I will offer is fishing the Missouri River in Montana primarily for rainbow trout and brown trout. I fished a nine-mile stretch of river between Holter Dam and Craig beginning in 1986 and continue to fish those waters today. The changes I have observed there are dramatic! In the late 1980s, I would see only one or two boats on the water and observe only half a dozen fishermen during a day's fishing. Now I commonly see over a dozen fishing boats on these waters and twenty or more other anglers are not uncommon. In addition, kayakers, canoers, and other paddlecraft are now common. The fishing is still good, according to my limited experience, but solitude is no longer available.

The third example is the Bighorn River in southern Montana. Crowding in the stretch of river below Yellowtail Dam near Fort Smith has increased dramatically over the years. In fact, many anglers complain of commercially guided fishing boats monopolizing the better pools on the river. The past practice has been for guides of paying anglers to use cell phones to call the next guided boat upriver and reveal that the downriver boat is about ready to vacate a pool and float downriver. The upstream boat then drifts down to the pool just as it is vacated and anchors there. In this way it becomes difficult for unguided anglers to access these pools.

While crowding issues are increasing for anglers, fishing does not seem to have as many access issues as hunting. This is mainly due to the navigable stream laws that permit public access to major waters in most states. Montana even has a stream access law that permits anglers to move up and down rivers and streams through private lands. The only requirement is that the stream be accessed through a publicly accessible area like a highway and that the angler remains below the high water mark.

My long-term view is that, while the problem of access and crowding for anglers is not as severe as for hunting, the problem is increasing for anglers. User conflicts nationwide involving jet skiers, rafters, canoers, and anglers and conflicts between wading anglers and boating anglers on western streams are but a few examples of this growing issue.

The Larger View

Lest these examples be taken as just the grumblings of an old, disillusioned biologist and sportsman, let's consider the larger view. According to the U.S. Bureau of Census (2012) the human population of the United States was approximately 76 million in 1900 and as of 2010 it was almost 309 million. That's a growth of 400 percent! This means that as a country we use more natural resources and we destroy more habitat, as our increasing human population needs new places to live, food to eat, energy, and water. I first became aware of the outcries of government wildlife agencies and many nonprofits about the loss of habitat when I was an aspiring wildlife biologist in college during the 1960s and 1970s. Fifty years of these outcries seem to have done nothing to stop our national population growth or the resulting increased pressures on our natural resources.

Jared Diamond (2011) authored the book *Collapse* in which he detailed the collapse of different societies. He describes societal collapses ranging historically from ancient Mayan cities to Easter Island's depopulation to the more current situations with Somalia and Rwanda. Diamond explains, ". . . different societies collapsed to different degrees and in somewhat different ways, while many societies didn't collapse at all." He poses the question, "When we deplete one resource (e.g., wood, oil, or ocean fish), can we count on being able to substitute some new resource (e.g., plastics, wind, and solar energy, or farmed fish)?" (Diamond 2011). Perhaps in the United States we can, but at what cost? Already we are seeing a major change in the quality of our consumptive outdoor recreational uses (hunting and fishing) due to the impacts of a growing human population!

Most Americans are blissfully unaware of these impacts on consumptive recreational activities or they don't care because it has not impacted them personally in a significant way. This is especially true for the urbanite or suburbanite whose only outdoor experiences may be going to the beach and an occasional camping trip to a state or national park. Those of us in the field of fish and wildlife are better positioned to see and understand the impacts of growth in human population. For better or worse, we are the prognosticators for the rest of our society.

Wildlife professionals learn in college the dangers of animal populations such as deer becoming too numerous. Fisheries biologists learn about the same population principles in pond management, where increasing fish numbers can lead to overpopulation. We study about the results of overpopulation where food sources are outstripped and disease and starvation result. In fact, this is the biological basis for much of the justification of regulated harvesting of fish and wildlife.

These same ecological principles that apply to overpopulations of animals also apply to the human animal. Yet seldom do natural resource professionals mention this human overpopulation problem occurring in the United States. I believe there are several reasons for this.

First, most professionals do not see any solution to the problem and thus find the problem "too big to address."

Second, many fisheries and wildlife professionals are employed by state or federal wildlife agencies, and numerous of the remaining professionals are employed by nonprofits. Government agencies are discouraged from entering into policy issues such as human population growth in the United States. That is not considered the purview of state or federal wildlife agencies. It is supposed to be a subject left to political figures and the political process. Politicians have understandably failed to address this issue. After all, addressing the nation's expanding human population brings into question such issues as immigration policies, individual rights to have as many children as desired, and birth control, including abortion. These are very controversial issues and dangerous for any politician to address.

Third, nonprofits do not have the restrictions of government agencies and can choose to address controversial issues. But doing so often brings opponents' retorts of calling such nonprofits "zealots" or "greenies" as a way to discount those concerns about human population increases. Also, there is the very real issue that most nonprofits have to rely on donations and contributions from the public for financial survival. Consequently, there is a very real pressure to be as non-controversial as possible in order to appeal to the most potential contributors.

The push back on attempts to raise interest in curtailing the nation's human population growth comes from those with interests in growth and "progress." This can be interpreted as interests in making money and economic gain. Almost all citizens want economic gains, but the trade-off is too often fewer natural resources and a declining quality of recreational experiences that depend on those natural resources. Most Americans who do not hunt or fish have not yet really experienced significant negative impacts on the quality of their outdoor encounters.

Unfortunately, the consumptive sports of hunting and angling are among the first of the outdoor sports to experience declines in quality. This is because crowding can be more of a problem for these participants. Those non-consumptive users visiting state or national parks or enjoying bird watching at a nature area do not seem to have the same concerns of crowding. For example, standing on a boardwalk and looking at an osprey through binoculars is an experience not greatly affected if several other people are engaged in the same activity. In fact, the discussion between the different onlookers can be part of the enjoyable experience.

But when elk hunting or turkey hunting for example, it is hard to enjoy the experience of trying to call an animal when several other hunters move in on the bugling elk or gobbling turkey and are competing for the same animal! The quality of the experience suffers. As another example, when hunting a field for upland birds, it is hard to enjoy a walk through a field that has just been hunted by a party of other hunters with dogs and they have flushed most of the birds out of the field.

Clearly, consumptive outdoor recreational pursuits such as hunting are much more competitive endeavors than non-consumptive outdoor recreational activities. This is why crowding is less tolerated by the consumptive user. Therefore, the consumptive outdoor sports of hunting and angling are more subject to declines in quality before any major effects are felt in the non-consumptive outdoor recreation arena. Those of us in the natural resource professions and the consumptive outdoor sports really have a responsibility to provide forewarnings to society. After all, we are among the first to see the negative impacts of our nation's expanding human population. We are the proverbial canaries in the coalmine.

Unfortunately, any coordinated nationwide effort to address the impacts of the interrelated issues of crowding, access, and human population growth are seriously hampered for state fish and wildlife agencies. Politically desiring to avoid conflictual issues is but one factor. The short tenure of state fish and wildlife agency directors, as mentioned before, creates an atmosphere where concern for reappointment in the short-term supersedes any actions on a controversial, long-term issue.

Ron Regan, executive director for the Association of Fish and Wildlife Agencies, (pers. comm.) states that, as of the writing of this book, only four directors of state fish and wildlife agencies have been a director for ten years or more. That means that forty-six state wildlife agency directors have served less than ten years as a director. This situation is primarily due to the high turnover rate of state directors because of their political appointment status and the changes incurred with each new governor elected in each state. This high turnover at the top makes it difficult to achieve any continuity in pursuing a national effort to address national population growth, access, crowding, changing trends, or any other long-term issues. It will take real leadership to address these kinds of issues, and it will require a society that has adaptive skills that allow them to withstand conflict, prevent work avoidance, and seek solutions as yet undefined.

What It Portends

Pat Graham (former Director of Montana Fish, Wildlife & Parks) tells the story of a U.S. Forest Service ranger that spent a month in the early 1900s on horseback in the Bob Marshall Wilderness of Montana. At the end of that adventure, the sum total of big game seen by the ranger was one mountain goat.

Even as our human population in the United States continues to increase, I do not foresee us returning to the low wildlife populations of the early 1900s. However, unless there are some brave souls who are willing to step forward and take the real risk of providing adaptive leadership in the areas of human population growth and private land access with all the ensuing conflicts in values and beliefs, then the current trends will continue.

I believe that there will continue to be hunting opportunities, although they will be more restrictive, with fewer harvest tags available and less private land open to public hunting. I foresee there will be a continued increase in leasing of private lands for hunting recreation and consequential increased closures to public access. Prices for access will continue to spiral upward. One will still be able to pick up a magazine and read about someone's successful big-game hunt or turn on the television, iPad, or other electronic device and watch someone enjoying a great hunt. The hunters showcased in these hunts will most likely be on an expensive, guided hunt to an area with very restricted access, or the lucky recipient of a hard-to-draw public land permit, or the owner/leasee of significant private lands. Most television shows I see about hunting already depend on exclusive private land access/ownership and/or on guides with leased lands.

The National Survey of Fishing, Hunting, and Wildlife-Associated Recreation (U.S. Dept. Interior et al. 2011) shows an increase of 5.7 million wildlife watchers between 2001 and 2011. This same time period has shown no significant increase in the numbers of hunters. What this means is a new world for state fish and wildlife agencies that will be very different from the past.

I believe state fish and wildlife agencies will face an increased danger of loss of public support for hunting as the numbers of hunters remain stagnant or decrease. As costs for access soar and public land hunting suffers from crowding, hunters will need to be from the more affluent levels of society and less from blue-collar America. I don't think the United States will become completely like the European system where hunting is primarily for the wealthy because, I hope, we will retain some large blocks of public lands in the forms of national forests and Bureau of Land Management lands. However, I believe that we will gradually move further along the spectrum toward a more European-system of hunting.

A number of readers may become upset at reading these predictions and reject my opinions. Rejection and anger are often efforts to forestall impending loss. It is a natural reaction, but it is also maladaptive behavior. Just because we don't like something doesn't mean it is not happening! Refuting or ignoring is just another way of avoiding the adaptive work needed to address the issues.

I challenge you to personally consider what **you** may be able to do to help society increase its adaptive capabilities, and what **you** may be able to do to conduct leadership activities on these important issues.

Challenges for State Fish and Wildlife Agencies

Relevancy—One of the immediate challenges facing most state fish and wildlife agencies is reestablishing their relevancy to the majority of Americans. As Jacobsen (2008) writes, "The biological and social context for wildlife management in the United States is transforming as the human population expands into and consumes wildlife habitat and citizens' interests and concerns about wildlife become increasingly diverse." In 2011, only 4.4 percent of the American public hunted and only 10.6 percent fished. Since three percent of the population both hunted and fished, the total number of citizens who either hunted or angled or both is approximately twelve percent of Americans (U.S. Dept. Interior et al. 2011). That leaves eighty-eight percent of Americans who do neither of these outdoor activities. Still, in the vast majority of states, the lion's share of state fish and wildlife agency funding is based upon sales of hunting and fishing licenses and taxes on hunting and fishing equipment. That is a problem of major proportions!

Wildlife watching involves 71.8 million citizens or twenty-three percent of the population. Yet, most states have not found a way to capitalize on funding from this segment of society. Wildlife belongs to **all** Americans, but most state fish and wildlife agencies have not found a way to improve their old funding models.

The Missouri Department of Conservation and the Arkansas Game and Fish Commission are exceptions because they have broadened their funding base by acquiring a percent of their state's annual sales tax. Colorado and Arizona are also examples of exceptions in that they have acquired funding through a percent of their state lottery annual revenues. Wyoming Game and Fish recently received funding from the state general funds to pay benefits for department personnel on the basis that those personnel were state employees. Despite these exceptions, the vast majority of state fish and wildlife agencies have not overcome their primary dependency on hunting and fishing related funding.

The consequence of most state fish and wildlife agencies relying on hunting and fishing generated revenues is that the focus of the agencies' efforts is on hunting and fishing management and services. That means that eighty-eight percent of the public has little connection to their state fish and wildlife agency. The relevancy of the agency is in doubt when it is perceived to serve only twelve percent of the public. This has been a continuous problem for many years—a symptom that this is another adaptive issue and will require adaptive leadership to solve.

I believe that there are two main reasons most states have not been able to broaden their funding sources. First, is that the problem has not been "ripened" with each state's publics. Hunting and fishing based revenues continue to support the state agencies at a level the general public finds acceptable.

Second, state agencies and their directors are often legally prevented from campaigning with the public for funding. Therefore, while agency directors bemoan the lack of funds, they feel their hands are tied or, at a minimum, they are reluctant to brave the dangerous waters of working with organizations outside government to push for funding. These are two of the main factors why the funding situation is stuck where it is.

Creating a sense of urgency among the general citizenry of each state will be required to move the situation forward and create change. This necessitates leadership and courage, not management acumen. As I mentioned in the chapter on leadership, the higher in the organization's hierarchy a person is, the more they have to lose if they take on the hazardous job of leading a change. That is why the higher you go in an organization, the less leadership you are likely to see.

Also, as mentioned previously, the tenure of directors in state fish and wildlife agencies is short, averaging less than three years. Thus, the focus of most directors is primarily short-term. It took the Arkansas Game and Fish Commission twelve years of work to get legislation passed in order to receive a percent of the state's sales tax funding (Steve Wilson, pers. comm.) This time frame is beyond the scope of most directors' tenure. What is required is courageous people stepping up and taking on the tough and hazardous leadership role to address this adaptive issue. So far, most of those in fish and wildlife agencies have not shown the courage to do this.

Access—This will continue to be a problem felt most acutely by hunters. The access issue is a classic adaptive issue involving conflicting, deeply held values and beliefs. On the landowner side are the values of landowner rights, and on the other side are the values of wildlife belonging to all Americans, and the North American model of conservation management in which equality of access to that wildlife is a major underpinning.

Broad questions for state fish and wildlife agencies include: *Should they, as government agencies, even intervene in this issue? Should state wildlife agencies' role be to just bend to whatever society evolves to require?* This may sound like heresy to a lot of biologists and hunters, but it is a political question that must be clearly answered for state fish and wildlife agencies to define their role in the access question. Perhaps the authors of the book *The Practice of Adaptive Leadership* (Heifetz, et. al. 2009) provided some insights into this dilemma when they stated:

> To build a sustainable world in an era of profound economic and environmental interdependence, each person, each country, each organization is challenged to sift through the wisdom and know-how of their heritage, to take the best from their histories, leave behind the lessons that no longer serve them, and innovate, not for change's sake, but for the sake of conserving and preserving the values and competence they find most essential and precious.

If state fish and wildlife agencies deem their role is to address the adaptive issue of access, then "ripening" the issue for landowners is one of the first steps. Currently, landowners have little incentive to allow public access for hunting. Why should they grant free access when there are hunters willing to pay?

State wildlife agencies and nonprofits have attempted to incent landowners through such programs as Montana's Department of Fish, Wildlife & Parks direct payments to landowners for access or through programs like Colorado Parks and Wildlife's providing big-game harvest tags to landowners which the landowners can then sell. These programs do provide some access, but they are a small drop in the ocean when you consider all the private lands closed to public hunting.

I don't have an answer for this issue. The good news is that, as with all adaptive issues, the answer does not exist until the stakeholders work out a solution with which they can all live. It is not a matter of selling "your" solution, but a matter of involving the stakeholders in an adaptive leadership process to develop a solution that everyone can accept.

If nothing is done to intervene and provide leadership to solve the adaptive issue of access, then the issue will continue to evolve through undiluted economics and the principles of supply and demand. The North American model's concept of equality of opportunity for recreation using the public's wildlife will continue to dissipate.

Human Population Growth—This is the 500-pound gorilla in the room. It will take great leadership and courage to address this issue on at least the national level, if not the international, or global, level. It will require taking on the huge forces that demand progress and growth at any cost. In the United States, this will even require a different national economic model than one based on continuous growth.

As I have stated previously, it will require addressing many deeply held values and conflicting beliefs, including those about abortion, the right to have as many children as desired, and immigration. I am not surprised that no one has stepped forward to provide leadership in these issues, especially since the task is so daunting. However, that does not mean that it is not a real adaptive problem and that it will not continue to impact America's quality of life unless it is addressed.

Jared Diamond in his book *Collapse* writes, "more than half of the world's original area of forest has already been converted to other uses, and at present conversion rates one-quarter of the forests that remain will become converted within the next half century" (Diamond 2011). Deforestation was one of the factors, if not the major factor, in all the collapses of past societies he describes in his book.

As many natural resource professionals are aware, "an even larger fraction of the world's wetlands than of its forests have already been destroyed, damaged, or converted" (Diamond 2011). Diamond uses a five-point framework of contributing factors for understanding societal collapse. He explains, "Four of those sets of factors—environmental damage, climate change, hostile neighbors, and friendly trade partners—may or may not prove significant for a particular society. The fifth set of factors—**the society's responses to its environmental problems**—**always proves significant**" (Diamond 2011). So why has the United States failed to address the impacts of its growing population?

Heifetz (1994) lists three reasons that societies fail to adapt to major issues.

1. They misperceive the nature of the threat.
2. Society may perceive the threat, but the challenge may exceed the culture's adaptive capability.
3. People resist the pain, anxiety, or conflict that accompanies a sustained effort to solve the problem.

I believe that all of these factors play some role in our nation's failure to address the implications of its growing population.

Citizens of this country either do not see the threat or ignore it. An early step is to raise awareness and concern over this issue (to ripen it). This will be no easy task and will likely require continued efforts over time. It will need to be approached like the current anti-smoking campaign in the United States.

Anti-smoking campaign efforts over many years have changed American society. I remember my uncles, father, and grandfather smoking in the 1950s and 1960s, along with most other adults I knew. The attitudes of smoking were slowly changed over the years by continuous anti-smoking campaign efforts so that today the attitudes and acceptance of smoking are very different than in my father's day. The Center for Disease Control states, "The anti-smoking campaign is a major public health success with few parallels in the history of public health" (Center for Disease Control 2015).

I believe that similar herculean efforts will be required to address this country's continued population growth. And that's just to get the issue ripened so that stakeholders with conflicting values will be willing to work together to address it.

I believe our nation does not yet have the cultural adaptive capability to successfully address this threat. **There is a need to build an adaptive culture among the citizens of this nation.** Most citizens have no clear idea of what that even means. It takes efforts that begin today to create a culture of raising sensitive problems (naming elephants in the room), sharing responsibility for the issue, acceptance and expectation of independent judgment, development of leadership capacity, and institutionalization of continuous learning.

Unfortunately these traits are seldom found in quantity within state fish and wildlife agency cultures or in government in general. Those cultures today remain ones of primarily conflict avoidance. Only when we have a more adaptive culture will people be willing to face the pain and anxiety of addressing the large adaptive issue of human population growth.

Lastly, skills in leading people to address adaptive issues will be paramount, as will be large doses of courage. Even when the skills may be present or acquirable, the item in shortest supply is often courage. I invite you to personally answer these three questions:

1. What are you committed to in the natural resource arena?
2. What can you learn about adaptive leadership skills to further that commitment?
3. How much courage do you have to address issues wisely and disappoint people at a level they can stand?

If you care about something but never take any action, the end result is the same as if you did not care at all! The famous English clergyman, Sidney Smith (1771-1845), once said, "It is the greatest of all mistakes to do nothing because you can only do little. . ." (Auden 2012).

Literature Cited

Adams, Kip and Matt Ross. 2015. QDMA's *Whitetail Report* 2015. Quality Deer Management Association. Bogart, GA. 59 pp.

Auden, W. H. 2012. *The Selected Writings of Sidney Smith*. Faber and Faber. London, UK. 416 pp.

Bullock, James. 2015. "The Importance of Private Lands to Wildlife." *Fair Chase* 31(2). pp 10.

Center for Disease Control and Prevention. 2015. http://www.cdc.gov/tobacco/data_statistics/sgr/history/

Diamond, Jared. 2011. *Collapse: How Societies Choose to Fail or Succeed*. Penguin Books. New York, NY. 589 pp.

Dickson, Tom. 2014. "Where Are All the Elk?" *Montana Outdoors*. Montana Fish, Wildlife & Parks. Helena, MT. Sept-Oct. issue. pp. 34-39.

Duda, Mark and Steven Bissell. 2000. "Bowhunting Participation, Trends, Satisfactions and Marketing Options." Responsive Management, Harrisonburg, VA. 23 pp.

Guynn, Dwight E. 1979. Management of Deer Hunters on Private Land in Colorado. Ph.D. Diss. Colorado State University, Fort Collins, Co. 253 pp.

____ and Marion K. Landry. 1997. "A Case Study of Citizen Participation as a Success Model for Innovative Solutions for Natural Resource Problems." *Wildlife Society Bulletin*. 25(2) pp. 392-398.

Heifetz, Ron, Alexander Grashow, and Marty Linsky. 2009. *The Practice of Adaptive Leadership*. Harvard Business Press. Boston, MA. 326 pp.

Jacobsen, Cynthia. 2008. *Wildlife Conservation and Management in the 21st Century: Understanding Challenges for Institutional Transformation*. Ph.D. Diss. Cornell University. Ithaca, NY. 147 pp.

Nickens, T. Edward. 2014. "Gobbler Positioning System." *Field and Stream*. May. pp. 58-62.

Senge, Peter M. 1990. *The Fifth Discipline*. Doubleday/Currency. New York, NY. 424 pp.

Shelby, Bo, T. A. Heberlein, J.J. Vaske, and G. Alfano. 1983. "Expectations, Preferences, and Feeling Crowded in Recreation Activities." *Leisure Sciences*. 6(1). pp. 1-14.

U.S. Census Bureau. 2012. *Statistical Abstract of the United States*. Washington, D.C. 1,406 pp.

U.S. Dept. of the Interior, U.S. Fish and Wildlife Service, and U.S. Dept. Commerce, U.S. Census Bureau. 2011. *National Survey of Fishing, Hunting, and Wildlife-Associated Recreation*. 161 pp.